Sweet Maria's

ITALIAN

DESSERTS

ST. MARTIN'S GRIFFIN ❦ NEW YORK

Sweet Maria's

ITALIAN DESSERTS

Classic and Casual Recipes for Cookies,
Cakes, Pastry, and Other Favorites

MARIA BRUSCINO SANCHEZ

Illustrations by Lizzy Rockwell

www.stmartins.com

Library of Congress Cataloging-in-Publication Data

Sanchez, Maria Bruscino.
    Sweet Maria's Italian desserts: classic and casual recipes for cookies, cakes, pastry, and other favorites / Maria Bruscino Sanchez.—1st ed.
      p.   cm.
    ISBN 0-312-24133-X
    1. Desserts—Italy. 2. Cookery, Italian. 3. Sweet Maria's (Bakery) I. Title.
TX773 .S293 2000
641.8'6'0945—dc21 00-040239

FIRST EDITION: September 2000

10 9 8 7 6 5 4 3 2 1

FOR EDGAR

WHO SHARES MY PASSION

FOR ALL THINGS ITALIAN

CONTENTS

ACKNOWLEDGMENTS

Thanks to Carla Glasser, my agent, for her generous encouragement;
Many thanks to my editor Marian Lizzi for her enthusiastic guidance;
For everyone at St. Martin's, thanks for your support and expertise;
Mille grazie to my parents for their constant faith in all my endeavors;
To the Sweet Maria's staff for their dedication, honesty, and humor:
Angela, Aunt Babe, Aunt Dolly, Gloria,
Joanne, Maryse, Sarah, Susan, and Vinny;
And especially to Grandma Bruscino, Aunt Giulia, Philomena, Gemma,
and all their families, for giving me an inspiring childhood and heritage.

INTRODUCTION

Italian desserts are as varied and delicious as Italy itself, and the journey of sweets from Italy to America has been a long and welcome one. Italian food has become one of the most popular cuisines in America not just for its fabulous flavor but for its simplicity. Italian-American homes are filled with a large variety of wonderful aromas, meat sauce, fried eggplant, and steamed artichokes. Fresh bread, amaretti, and roasted chestnuts also fill the air.

Growing up in an American Italian home, we didn't eat dessert on a daily basis. A simple everyday Italian dessert is a piece of fruit, a slice of cheese, and a handful of nuts. Sure, there was always a biscotti in the cookie jar for snacks, but the real cakes, pies, and puddings were reserved for Sundays and other holiday celebrations. Sunday dinners and holidays meant all the generations coming together to share a meal, and a special dessert, which is typical both in Italian and Italian-American homes.

Many traditional Italian desserts, such as pannetone and rice pies, are made to celebrate important Roman Catholic holidays, such as Christmas and Easter. The ingredients themselves—ricotta cheese, rice, flour, and spices—are staples of Italian life. Fresh ingredients are a vital part to all Italian cooking, especially desserts. The flexibility of Italian cooks to substitute one fruit or nut for another based on availability is something to be admired. My mom always talks about "making do" with what you have. This philosophy is a creative way to cook. All the ingredients used in this book are readily available in most supermarkets, and you can also "make do" as you wish.

This book is a collection of various Italian sweets. Cookies have always been a part of family functions, and are perhaps the best-known Italian desserts. Every baker has his or her specialty. In our family, we would all bake one batch of our favorite and then pool them all together to create spectacular trays for weddings and showers. These cookies also make a great snack throughout the day and even at breakfast.

Italian cakes and pies are casual and delicious. They are not heavily iced and decorated as American layer cakes are. Italians are also known for their pastry such as cannoli and pasticiotta. While these are often purchased at a favorite bakery, I've included these recipes for those who would like to try them. Other classic desserts, such as tiramisù and panna cotta, are delicious and easy to prepare.

Some of the traditional family recipes in this book were handed down as "a handful of this" and "a handful of that." Luckily, my mom and I followed my grandmother around the kitchen with a measuring cup, insisting she measure her handfuls. It was a nuisance then, three women in one kitchen, but I'm sure she would be proud to share her rice pie recipe and the others presented here.

This collection is not a region-by-region account of traditional desserts. Traditions and food vary widely throughout Italy. My family is Neapolitan and Abruzzese and my husband's family is Sicilian, so many of the recipes reflect these regions. Some of these recipes are classics that I've updated or recipes that are inspired by traveling through Italy. Many are favorites enjoyed by my customers at Sweet Maria's Bakery, where Italian-Americans and others purchase desserts that range from traditional to contemporary.

The sights, food, and spirit of Italy and its people are truly enlightening. I hope you'll enjoy making these sweets, as well as eating them, and will be encouraged to preserve your own family traditions through great food and delicious desserts.

INGREDIENTS

Flour

It's very important that you use the right type of flour for each cake, cookie, bread, and pie. Each recipe will specify the best type of flour to be used, but here are general guidelines:

CAKES: Cake flour works best for delicate fine-crumb layer cakes and sponge cakes. This flour is generally lighter and "less strong" than all-purpose flour. It will give your cakes a fine texture. In contrast, some of the cakes in this book are rustic, casual cakes that are generally filled with nuts and dried fruit. These use all-purpose flour. All-purpose flour will give your batter a bit more strength to hold up the fruit and nuts. Otherwise, the fruit and nuts will sink to the bottom of the cake.

PIES AND TARTS: All-purpose or unbleached flour is fine for most of the crusts used in this book. A basic *pasta frolla,* or sweet crust recipe, is used for many of the tarts and pies.

COOKIES: All-purpose or unbleached flour is used for many of the cookies and biscuits.

BREADS: You can use all-purpose or unbleached flour for the sweet bread recipes.

Sugar

SUPERFINE GRANULATED SUGAR: Best for all of these recipes, it has a nice fine grain that allows it to blend well with other ingredients.

CONFECTIONERS' SUGAR: This very finely processed sugar with a bit of cornstarch added to prevent any clumping is used for many icings and glazes. It is graded according to how fine it is ground. "10-x" is the most widely found confectioners' sugar.

BROWN SUGAR: Regular granulated sugar that has been processed with molasses. It adds a particularly rich flavor to your baked goods.

Eggs

Whenever eggs are used in a recipe, they are Grade A large eggs. For cake baking it is important to use eggs that are brought to room temperature. If you need to separate eggs, it's easier to do when they are cold, so consider doing this ahead of time.

Butter

Fresh unsalted butter really can't be beat for flavor and texture. Using unsalted allows you to control the amount of salt in the recipe.

Vegetable Oil

Many of these Italian treats are fried pastries. Use a vegetable oil for any frying. Olive oil is not only expensive, but a bit too flavorful for most of these sweets.

Vegetable Shortening

If shortening is called for, use an all-vegetable shortening. To melt shortening, place in a small saucepan over low heat. Stir until melted. Or microwave on low until melted. Let cool before adding to other ingredients.

Nuts

Many common nuts are used in these recipes, such as almonds, walnuts, hazelnuts, and chestnuts. If pine nuts (pignoli) and pistachio nuts are hard to find, try an Italian or Middle Eastern import shop. If you purchase a large quantity, you can store the leftover nuts in the freezer. Simply wrap in heavy-duty plastic freezer bags. Chop the nuts right before you begin a recipe.

Toasting the nuts brings out their natural oils and flavors. Simply place desired amount of nuts in a single layer on a parchment-lined cookie sheet. Bake at 350°F for 5 to 8 minutes, or until lightly browned. Let cool before using.

To coarsely chop nuts, use a cutting board and a sharp straight knife.

To finely chop nuts, use a food processor and pulse to desired fineness. Nuts should resemble coarse salt.

Baking Powder and Baking Soda

Be sure to use a fresh supply of both baking powder and baking soda in all your baking. Store unused portions in airtight containers at room temperature.

Yeast

For the sweet bread recipes in this book, use an active dry yeast, available in most supermarkets. Because dry yeast needs warmth and moisture to activate its leavening power, many of the recipes direct you to dissolve the yeast in lukewarm water before adding it to the dough. Water that is too hot will kill the yeast and water that is too cold will not activate it. Store unused unopened yeast packages in the refrigerator.

Spices

Italian desserts use spices such as cinnamon, nutmeg, and ground cloves. Most of these spices are available in supermarkets. Be sure your supply is fresh to provide the fullest flavor.

Extracts and Liqueurs

Pure extracts and high-quality liqueurs and wines add flavor to your desserts. If you want the best result, don't skimp with imitation flavors. Some common flavors include vanilla, marsala wine, amaretto, and rum.

Fruit Rinds

Abundant in Italy and full of fresh flavor, the rinds of citrus fruit such as lemons and oranges are very popular in Italian desserts. To grate the rind, use a zester or four-sided grater. Be sure to avoid the bitter white pith underneath the rind. To juice citrus fruits, start with the fruit at room temperature.

Fruit

Many types of fruit are used in these desserts, including apples, pears, figs, plums, assorted berries, and cherries. Every baker has his or her favorite; I generally use McIntosh or Granny Smith apples, Bosc for pears, and a variety of berries. With so much produce available year-round these days, it's easy to find a good assortment. If you can't find fresh raspberries or blueberries, try using an "IQF" product. These are berries that are "individually quick frozen" separately, then frozen together. The whole berry can be thawed and added to the dessert without breaking into pieces. The fruit can also provide a bit of juice as it thaws.

Chocolate and Cocoa

Both semisweet baking bars and cocoa are used to flavor the chocolate desserts in this book. Be sure to use the freshest, highest-quality chocolate available. Dutch process cocoa provides a rich chocolate flavor and color.

Cheese

Served with fruit, cheese is an Italian dessert in itself, so it's no surprise there are many Italian desserts that feature cheese. Some of the favorites are:

MASCARPONE: This soft Italian cheese is like cream cheese and is best known for its use in tiramisù.

RICOTTA: This soft cheese with a slightly sweet flavor is used in classic Italian desserts such as cannoli, Easter pies, and cheesecakes. Use fresh whole milk ricotta, not the low-fat kind made from skim milk. You may need to experiment with different brands of ricotta. The moisture content will vary among manufacturers. Try to use a firm, less watery brand, if available.

Heavy Cream

Use heavy cream when making whipped cream for a frosting or a garnish. This rich cream has the highest percentage of butterfat. Pasteurized cream is the freshest-tasting cream but is usually hard to find. Ultra-pasteurized cream, the most widely available heavy cream, works fine in these recipes.

When using whipped cream for a cake frosting, be sure to whip it until stiff, as the recipe directs. To garnish a slice of cake or pie with a dollop of cream, it can be a little less stiff.

EQUIPMENT

Many of the tools you'll need for these recipes are the usual spatulas, knives, mixing bowls, and rolling pins that most of us have on hand. Here are a few other things you may need.

Mixers

There are two types of mixers a well-equipped kitchen should have: Hand-held mixers are ideal when you need to beat ingredients over the top of a double boiler. A stand-up mixer is the best choice for most other situations because you can walk away and do another task while the mixer mixes.

Parchment

Baking parchment is a vital tool for baking. You can find it in most supermarkets or gourmet kitchen and party shops. Use it to line cookie sheets as well as cake pans. It eliminates messy greasing of pans and makes cleanup easy. For cake pans, cut parchment into circles to fit the bottom of the pan you're using. Cut 2-inch-wide strips of parchment. Spray the cake pan with a nonstick spray, then line the bottom of the pan with the circle and place the strips of parchment along the sides. Line layer-cake pans as well as loaf pans, tube pans, and springform pans in the same way.

Cookie Sheets

Use sturdy, straight, clean sheets for cookie baking.

Cake Pans

Use sturdy straight-sided pans for cake baking. These include loaf pans and tube pans. Disposable foil pans are not recommended. Springform pans are used for several of the cakes in this book. Popular for cheesecakes, they have a removable bottom and spring mechanism that allows you to remove the cake from the pan without breaking it. If you're taking the cake to a party and don't want to use the metal bottom plate, cut a circle of corrugated cardboard to fit the bottom of the pan. Cover with foil and press into place as a disposable pan bottom.

Tart and Pie Pans

Many of the tarts in this book use a 9-inch round tart pan with removable bottom. This makes serving easy and creates a professional presentation. For pies, these recipes use a 9-inch round deep-dish pie pan. I like the glass Pyrex pans so I can check out the bottom crust.

Ovens

The recipes in this book are timed in a conventional oven, either gas or electric. If you are using a convection oven your baking time will be less.

Because baking is very sensitive, it's important to check your oven temperature. Invest in an inexpensive oven thermometer to be sure your temperature is accurate. You may need to call a repairman just to make an adjustment.

Although I don't recommend going out to buy a new oven, I love my glass oven door and oven lights. I always like to see how the baking is progressing without opening the door, which would allow the heat to escape; this can cause breads and cakes to collapse.

Cannoli Tubes

These are hollow metal rods, about 6 inches long, that are used to form the shell of the cannoli. You can find these at many specialty kitchen shops. The dough is wrapped around the rod, secured with egg white, and deep fried. After cooling, grab the rod with your fingertips and gently twist and pull to remove the shell. Reuse as necessary.

Fluted Pastry Cutter

This tool is similar to a pizza cutter but provides a small scalloped edge to many of the desserts in this book. You can use a pizza cutter or sharp straight knife instead, but you won't have the fancy edge.

Wire Cooling Racks

Every baker should have a few wire cooling racks. Place hot baked goods on the racks to cool. This allows air to circulate underneath to cool evenly and completely. Use wire racks to frost cookies and sweet breads. Just place a sheet of parchment or wax paper underneath to catch any excess frosting.

Double Boiler

A double boiler is used to melt chocolate slowly or cook delicate custards over simmering water. If you don't have a double boiler, use a saucepan filled with water as your bottom, and a wide-mouthed stainless steel bowl on top.

BASIC BAKING TECHNIQUES

Each recipe will give you tips on mixing, baking, and storing your desserts. Here are just a few guidelines about some of the commonly used terms you'll see throughout the book.

Making a "Well"

I use this technique often. When dry ingredients are combined in a bowl, make a mound, and with a wooden spoon make a hole on top of the mound. This is your "well." In a separate bowl, mix the wet ingredients. Pour these into the well and mix together.

Turning Out Dough

I use this technique when the dough gets too heavy for hand mixing or electric mixing. Simply empty contents of mixing bowl onto a lightly floured surface such as your counter or table. Knead together with your hands to form a soft dough.

Folding the Egg Whites

For many cake batters, the egg whites are whipped separately until stiff. Use small, light-handed strokes, with a rubber spatula, to turn whites into other batter. This will blend air into the batter. Be sure to scrape the bottom of the bowl so that all batter is incorporated evenly.

Filling a Pastry Bag

Pastry bags are used for a few cookie recipes in this book. An easy way to fill a pastry bag is to place the bag tip side down in a tall drinking glass. Fold the top edges over the sides of the glass. This will allow the bag to stay open while you spoon batter or frosting into the bag. Be careful not to overfill. Gather up edges of bag and remove from glass. Squeeze and add desired pressure to the middle of the bag to release frosting or batter from the tip.

Dusting and Rolling in Confectioners' Sugar

Many Italian cakes and pastries have a simple dusting of powdered sugar as a garnish. Place a few tablespoons of confectioners' sugar in a small dry strainer. Hold the strainer over the cake or pastry. With a teaspoon, stir the sugar to dust.

To coat cookies with confectioners' sugar, place a small amount of sugar in a medium-size mixing bowl. Place 10 to 12 cookies at a time in the sugar. Use two spoons or your hands to carefully toss and coat the cookies, being sure not to break them.

Baking Desserts for Company

Entertaining can be stressful. When baking or cooking for company, try to use a recipe you're familiar with and that you've made before. This eliminates some of the stress. Try a dry run a week or two ahead of your scheduled party to make sure you're comfortable with the recipe.

Many of the desserts in this book, especially the cakes, have several components, many of which can be made ahead. If you're having company on a Saturday evening, bake the cake and make the fillings on Friday. Assemble on Saturday morning and serve on Saturday night.

A Few Tips on Frying

Several of the desserts in this book are delicious fried pastries. To make them properly, it's important that the oil be medium hot. If it becomes too hot, the pastries will be too brown on the outside and raw on the inside. If the oil is not hot enough, the pastries will turn out soggy and pale. To turn pastries in oil, use two forks or a slotted spoon. To remove pastries from oil, use a slotted spoon and place on absorbent paper to drain. Fried pastries taste best when they're freshly fried.

COOKIES

◆　◆　◆

Because cookies are so vital to Italian-American celebrations, they are a large part of this book. Cookie trays are found at most parties, and certain types of cookies are baked for specific occasions such as weddings, Christmas, and Easter. Even when most people say they don't have room for dessert, they usually make room for a cookie.

Italian cookies are generally plain biscuits, enjoyed throughout the year, ideal for dessert with fruit or ice cream, or a simple snack or breakfast. Cookies that are baked for specific holidays, like Christmas and Easter, are usually richer and fancier, using dried fruit, nuts, and raisins.

Italian cookies traditionally have less fat than American cookies. This makes them more like biscuits and harder in texture. I've included some of these cookies as well as variations that are more like American cookies with a bit more butter. Here are a few tips on the types of cookies that follow.

Drop Cookies

These are the easiest type of cookie to make. After mixing the dough, simply use a teaspoon to drop the dough onto a parchment-lined cookie sheet.

Rolled Cookies

This is another simple cookie, formed by rolling the dough into balls. If the dough is a bit sticky, dust your fingers lightly with flour.

Rolled and Filled Cookies

These cookies are rolled with a rolling pin. For most of them, the dough should be chilled first for easier rolling. You can usually make the dough ahead and refrigerate overnight. Finish the filling (usually jelly, nuts, and spices) and bake the next day.

When you're rolling and cutting dough, save all your scraps to roll at the end. By adding scraps to the fresh dough you can toughen it. While rolling, store unused portion of dough in the refrigerator to keep chilled.

When using cookie cutters, dust them lightly with flour to eliminate sticking.

Biscotti

These are popular Italian cookies that are baked twice. The dough is formed into long thin loaves and baked. After cooling, the loaves are diagonally sliced into ½-inch slices. They are baked again for a toasted crunchy cookie.

Bar Cookies

Bar cookies are another easy-to-make cookie and look great on a cookie tray. The dough is pressed into a baking pan, baked, cooled, and cut into squares or strips. You can also cut them into triangles, strips, or diamond shapes.

JELLY AND NUT CRESCENTS

These are a fancy holiday treat that can be made with any flavor jelly.
I love them with raspberry filling for the holidays, not just for their flavor
but for the way they dress up a holiday cookie tray.

CRUST:

¼ POUND BUTTER, SOFTENED	1 EGG YOLK
3 OUNCES CREAM CHEESE, SOFTENED	1 CUP FLOUR

FILLING:

½ CUP BROWN SUGAR	½ TEASPOON CINNAMON
1 CUP WALNUTS, FINELY CHOPPED	¾ CUP JELLY, ANY FLAVOR

1. In an electric mixer, cream the butter and cream cheese until light and fluffy. Add yolk. Mix until well blended. Gradually add flour on low speed. Turn out dough onto a lightly floured surface.

2. Knead until well blended. Divide dough in half. Wrap in plastic and refrigerate for 2 to 3 hours or overnight.

3. Preheat oven to 375°F.

4. In a small bowl, mix brown sugar, walnuts, and cinnamon. Set aside.

5. Using a lightly floured rolling pin and surface, roll out one half of dough until ⅛ inch thick. Spread half the jelly onto dough in a thin layer. Sprinkle with half the sugar and cinnamon mixture.

6. Using a fluted pastry cutter, cut the dough into 12 wedges.

7. Roll each edge, starting at the wide end, toward the center of the circle. Place on a parchment-lined cookie sheet and slightly curve each cookie into a crescent. Space cookies about 2 inches apart. Repeat rolling and filling with remaining dough.

8. Bake for 15 to 20 minutes, or until golden brown.

9. Remove the cookie sheet from the oven. Using a metal spatula, place cookies on a wire cooling rack. Cool. Store cookies in an airtight container.

YIELD: 24 COOKIES

EGG YOLK BISCUITS

These biscuits are perfect for breakfast or a snack. This version is a plain vanilla cookie brushed with egg yolk before baking. The recipe is also flexible: You can flavor the dough with lemon, orange, or almond instead of vanilla extract. Because these cookies are sturdy, use them for the bottom layer of your cookie tray.

½ POUND BUTTER	2½ CUPS FLOUR
1 CUP SUGAR	1 TEASPOON BAKING POWDER
3 EGG YOLKS	2 TABLESPOONS MILK
2 TEASPOONS VANILLA	

1. In an electric mixer, cream butter and sugar until light. Add 2 egg yolks and vanilla. Beat until well mixed. On low speed, add flour, baking powder, and milk. Mix just until blended. Turn out dough onto a lightly floured surface. Knead until smooth. Wrap in plastic wrap and refrigerate for 2 to 3 hours or overnight.

2. Preheat oven to 350°F.

3. Roll out dough on a lightly floured surface until ¼ inch thick. Using a cookie cutter or rim of a juice glass, cut into circles about 2½ inches in diameter.

4. Place cookies on a parchment-lined cookie sheet, spacing them 2 inches apart.

5. Brush tops of cookies with remaining egg yolk and sprinkle with sugar.

6. Bake for 15 to 20 minutes, or until lightly browned.

7. Remove cookie sheet from the oven. Using a metal spatula, remove cookies from the cookie sheet and place on wire cooling rack. Cool.

8. Store unused cookies in an airtight container.

YIELD: 24 COOKIES

ORANGE DROP COOKIES
ANGINETTI D'ARANCIA

These light and flavorful cookies are always a favorite. This recipe uses a fresh orange flavor, a nice variation on the traditional lemon version. They are quite tasty topped with an orange confectioners' icing. After the icing is dry, stack these cookies in a large mound on top of a tiered cake plate for a fabulous wedding or shower sweet.

¼ POUND BUTTER, SOFTENED	GRATED RIND OF 1 ORANGE
½ CUP SUGAR	3 CUPS FLOUR
3 EGGS	3 TEASPOONS BAKING POWDER
½ CUP ORANGE JUICE	

1. Preheat oven to 350°F.

2. In an electric mixer, cream the butter and sugar until light. Add eggs, orange juice, and orange rind. Mix until well blended.

3. On low speed, gradually add the flour and baking powder. Mix just until blended.

4. Using a teaspoon, drop rounded teaspoons onto a lightly greased cookie sheet, spacing each cookie about 2 inches apart.

5. Bake for 8 to 10 minutes, or until lightly browned.

6. Remove from the oven. Using a metal spatula, remove cookies from the sheet onto a wire cooling rack. Cool completely. Frost with orange confectioners' icing (see following recipe).

YIELD: ABOUT 50 COOKIES

ORANGE CONFECTIONERS' ICING

This versatile icing can be made with almost any flavor. Simply substitute water for orange juice and add 2 teaspoons of extract. This version really accents the orange flavor of the anginetti.

6 CUPS CONFECTIONERS' SUGAR   **¾ CUP ORANGE JUICE**
GRATED RIND OF 1 ORANGE

1. In an electric mixer on medium speed, beat all ingredients until smooth.

2. Using a metal spatula, frost the tops of the cookies. The frosting will drip down the sides of the cookie. Dry the frosted cookies on a wire cooling rack. Place a sheet of parchment or wax paper underneath cooling rack to catch excess frosting. Store in an airtight container.

YIELD: ENOUGH FOR 50 COOKIES

LENTEN BISCUITS

QUARESIMALI

These plain biscuits are usually baked during the Lenten season. Because they use the traditional method of biscotti baking, without fat, be sure to slice them while they're still warm. If you let them cool first, they'll be too hard to slice.

2 CUPS FLOUR	1 CUP SLICED ALMONDS
½ CUP BROWN SUGAR	2 TEASPOONS CINNAMON
1 TEASPOON BAKING POWDER	3 EGGS
PINCH OF SALT	¼ CUP MILK

1. Preheat oven to 375°F.

2. In a large bowl, combine flour, brown sugar, baking powder, salt, almonds, and cinnamon. Make a well in the center. Set aside.

3. In a separate bowl, mix eggs and milk with a wire whisk. Add the egg mixture to the well. Stir with a wooden spoon. Turn out dough onto a lightly floured surface and knead until dough is blended.

4. Divide dough in half. Roll into two loaves, about 12 inches long. Place the loaves on a parchment-lined cookie sheet, spacing them 3 inches apart.

5. Bake for 20 to 25 minutes, or until golden brown.

6. Remove cookie sheet from the oven.

7. Carefully remove hot loaves from the cookie sheet and place on a cutting board. While still warm, cut the loaves diagonally into ½-inch-wide slices.

8. Place slices in a single layer on a cookie sheet. Return to the oven for 15 to 20 minutes, or until lightly browned. Remove cookie sheet from the oven. Cool toasted biscotti on wire cooling rack. Store in an airtight container.

YIELD: 24 COOKIES

ALMOND MERINGUES

*These crunchy dry biscuits are sometimes called "forgotten cookies," because they
bake in the oven for a long time at a slow temperature. They are a treat served alone,
or piled with berries and whipped cream. You can make them any size,
but I prefer these sweet little kisses formed with a pastry bag.*

4 EGG WHITES
1¼ CUPS SUGAR

½ TEASPOON ALMOND EXTRACT

1. Preheat oven to 225°F.

2. In an electric mixer with whisk attachment, beat egg whites until soft peaks form.
   Gradually add sugar and almond extract. Beat until stiff.

3. Fill a pastry bag (without a tip) with half the meringue dough. Pipe small kisses
   onto a parchment-lined cookie sheet. You can pipe them close together because
   they don't spread when baking. Refill pastry bag with remaining dough and pipe
   until finished.

4. Bake for 1½ hours, or until dry.

5. Remove cookies from the oven. Cool meringues on parchment. When cool, carefully remove from parchment with a metal spatula. Store unused meringues in
   plastic wrap at room temperature.

YIELD: ABOUT 50 SMALL COOKIES

VARIATION: COCOA ALMOND MERINGUES

Enjoy these cookies on their own or use them festively to cover our
Mandarin Orange Meringue Cake (see page 72).

4 EGG WHITES

1 CUP SUGAR

3 TABLESPOONS COCOA

½ TEASPOON ALMOND EXTRACT

Follow directions for almond meringues, beating in cocoa after sugar. Bake at 225°F for 1½ hours, or until dry.

◆ HOW TO MAKE A COOKIE TRAY ◆

START WITH A FLAT AND STURDY PLATE OR BASKET. LINE WITH A DOILY. START STACKING COOKIES, PLACING THE MORE DURABLE COOKIES, SUCH AS BISCOTTI, ON THE BOTTOM OF THE TRAY. CONTINUE TO STACK A VARIETY OF FLAVORS IN DECREASING ORDER TO FORM A PYRAMID. PLACE FRAGILE JELLY-FILLED COOKIES ON TOP. WRAP IN CELLOPHANE AND TIE WITH RIBBONS.

SWEET SPICE COOKIES

These tasty little drop cookies are loaded with chocolate chips, nuts, and cinnamon—
a delicious combination and one of my favorite take-to-school lunch treats.

½ POUND BUTTER, SOFTENED	PINCH OF SALT
1 CUP BROWN SUGAR	1 TEASPOON CINNAMON
3 EGGS	2 CUPS CHOPPED WALNUTS
2 CUPS FLOUR	1 CUP CHOCOLATE CHIPS
1 TEASPOON BAKING SODA	

1. Preheat oven to 350°F.

2. In an electric mixer, cream butter and brown sugar until light. Add eggs. Mix until well blended. On low speed, gradually add flour, baking soda, salt, and cinnamon. Mix just until blended.

3. Stir in nuts and chocolate chips.

4. Using a teaspoon, drop dough onto a parchment-lined cookie sheet, spacing each cookie about 2 inches apart.

5. Bake for 12 to 15 minutes, or until golden brown. Remove cookie sheet from the oven. Using a metal spatula, remove cookies from cookie sheet and place on a wire cooling rack. Cool completely. Store unused cookies in an airtight container.

YIELD: 50 COOKIES

RICOTTA DROP COOKIES
BISCOTTI DI RICOTTA

These moist cookie drops combine two popular flavors for Italian desserts, ricotta and lemon. This combination is especially popular in the Neapolitan region, where both ingredients are plentiful. It's hard to travel anywhere in southern Italy without seeing endless groves of citrus trees.

¼ POUND BUTTER, SOFTENED	GRATED RIND OF 1 LEMON
1 CUP SUGAR	2 CUPS FLOUR
1 EGG	½ TEASPOON BAKING SODA
¼ CUP RICOTTA	PINCH OF SALT

1. Preheat oven to 350°F.

2. In an electric mixer, cream butter and sugar until light. Add egg, ricotta, and lemon rind. Mix until well blended. On low speed, add flour, baking soda, and salt. Mix just until blended.

3. Drop dough from a rounded teaspoon onto a parchment-lined cookie sheet, spacing each cookie about 2 inches apart.

4. Bake for 10 to 15 minutes, or until lightly browned. Remove cookie sheet from the oven. Use a metal spatula to transfer cookies to a wire cooling rack. Cool completely.

5. Dust with confectioners' sugar. Serve cooled. Store unused cookies in an airtight container.

YIELD: 30 COOKIES

FIG AND WALNUT BISCOTTI

Perfect dunked in wine or espresso, these hearty biscuits have a shiny professional look from the beaten egg brushed on top. Because they stay fresh for so long, they're the perfect cookie to bake and keep in the cookie jar.

1½ CUPS FLOUR

2 TEASPOONS BAKING POWDER

1 CUP SUGAR

2 TEASPOONS CINNAMON

½ TEASPOON SALT

⅔ CUP WALNUT HALVES

⅔ CUP COARSELY CHOPPED DRIED FIGS

2 EGGS

2 TEASPOONS VANILLA

1 EGG FOR EGG WASH

1. Preheat oven to 375°F.

2. In a large bowl, combine flour, baking powder, sugar, cinnamon, salt, walnuts, and figs. Stir until blended. Make a well in the center.

3. In a separate bowl, mix the 2 eggs and vanilla with a wire whisk. Add the eggs to the well. Stir with a wooden spoon. Turn out dough onto a lightly floured surface. Knead until dough is blended.

4. Divide dough in half. Roll into two loaves, about 12 inches long. Place the loaves on a parchment-lined cookie sheet, spacing them 3 inches apart.

5. In a small bowl, beat remaining egg with a fork. Using a pastry brush, brush the beaten egg on top of the loaves.

6. Bake for 20 to 25 minutes, or until golden brown.

7. Remove from the oven.

8. Carefully remove hot loaves from the cookie sheet and place on a cutting board. While warm, slice the loaves diagonally into ½-inch-wide slices.

9. Place slices in a single layer on the cookie sheet. Return to oven for 15 to 20 minutes, or until lightly browned. Remove cookie sheet from the oven. Cool toasted biscotti on wire cooling rack. Store in an airtight container.

YIELD: ABOUT 25 COOKIES

ORANGE CLOVE BISCOTTI

These biscotti are a classic pairing of citrus and spice. They are one of the first cookies I learned to bake with my mom. They're perfect partners to a tall glass of iced cappuccino or a few scoops of chocolate ice cream.

¼ POUND BUTTER, SOFTENED	2½ CUPS FLOUR
1 CUP SUGAR	1½ TEASPOONS BAKING POWDER
2 EGGS	1½ TEASPOONS GROUND CLOVES
GRATED RIND OF 2 ORANGES	
JUICE OF 1 ORANGE	

1. Preheat oven to 350°F.

2. In an electric mixer, cream the butter and sugar until light. Add eggs, orange rind, and orange juice. Mix until well blended. On low speed, add flour, baking powder, and cloves. Mix just until blended.

3. Turn out dough onto a lightly floured surface. Divide dough into thirds. Roll into three loaves, about 12 inches long. Place on a parchment-lined cookie sheet, spacing each 3 inches apart.

4. Bake for 20 to 25 minutes, or until lightly browned.

5. Remove cookie sheet from the oven. Using two metal spatulas, carefully place loaves on wire cooling racks. Cool.

6. Place cooled loaves on a cutting board. Using a large sharp knife, cut diagonally into ½-inch slices.

7. Place slices on the cookie sheet in a single layer. Bake for 12 to 15 minutes, or until lightly browned. Remove cookies from the oven. Cool toasted biscotti on wire cooling racks. Store in an airtight container.

YIELD: 30 COOKIES

MOLASSES NUT SLICES

These cookies have a rich molasses flavor, perfect with a glass of cold milk. They are so easy to make—just roll into loaves, refrigerate, cut, and bake. When I was a child, these cookies always reminded me of slices of pepperoni.

½ POUND BUTTER, SOFTENED

½ CUP SUGAR

2 TABLESPOONS MOLASSES

1 EGG

2 CUPS FLOUR

1 TEASPOON BAKING POWDER

¾ CUP CHOPPED WALNUTS

1. In an electric mixer, cream butter and sugar until light. Add molasses and egg. Blend until well mixed. On low speed, gradually add flour, baking powder, and nuts. Turn out dough onto a lightly floured surface.

2. Divide dough in half. Roll each piece into a cylinder about 1½ inches wide. Wrap in plastic wrap and refrigerate for 2 to 3 hours or overnight.

3. Preheat oven to 375°F.

4. Place dough cylinders on a cutting board. Cut dough into slices about ½ inch wide. Place on parchment-lined cookie sheet, spacing each 2 inches apart.

5. Bake for 15 to 20 minutes, or until lightly browned. Remove from the oven.

6. Use a metal spatula to remove cookies to a wire cooling rack. Cool completely.

7. Store in an airtight container.

YIELD: 40 COOKIES

AMARETTI

These classic Italian almond macaroons are very popular. To roll the cookies
more easily, dip your fingers into a bowl of water. This will prevent
the dough from sticking to your hands.
In Sicily, amaretti cookies are formed into mounds with a crater on top,
dusted with confectioners' sugar, and baked, so that they resemble
Mount Etna. My version is shaped in the more traditional cookie manner,
but is dusted with confectioners' sugar too.

½ POUND ALMOND PASTE, BROKEN
INTO SMALL PIECES

½ CUP SUGAR

¼ CUP FLOUR

½ CUP CONFECTIONERS' SUGAR

1 EGG

ADDITIONAL CONFECTIONERS' SUGAR
TO GARNISH

1. Preheat oven to 350°F.

2. In an electric mixer, combine almond paste, sugar, flour, and confectioners' sugar. Mix on low speed until blended. Add egg. Mix on low speed for 2 minutes. This will make a sticky dough.

3. Roll dough into 1-inch balls. Place on parchment-lined cookie sheet, spacing them 2 inches apart. Using your fingers, press down the tops gently to flatten slightly. Dust the tops of cookies with additional confectioners' sugar.

4. Bake for 15 to 20 minutes, or until golden brown. Remove the cookie sheet from the oven. Let cookies cool completely on parchment for easiest removal. When cookies are completely cooled, use a metal spatula to loosen them from the parchment. Store in an airtight container.

YIELD: 20 COOKIES

CHOCOLATE HAZELNUT BISCOTTI
BISCOTTI DI CIOCCOLATA CON NOCI

Chocolate lovers adore these rich biscotti with toasted hazelnuts. For the richest flavor, use a Dutch process cocoa and freshly toasted hazelnuts.

¼ POUND BUTTER, SOFTENED

¾ CUP SUGAR

2 TABLESPOONS HAZELNUT LIQUEUR

2 EGGS

2 CUPS FLOUR

½ CUP COCOA, PREFERABLY DUTCH PROCESS

2 TEASPOONS BAKING POWDER

¾ CUP HAZELNUTS, CHOPPED AND TOASTED

1. Preheat oven to 350°F.

2. In an electric mixer, cream butter and sugar until light. Add hazelnut liqueur and eggs. Mix until well blended.

3. On low speed, gradually add flour, cocoa, and baking powder. Stir in hazelnuts.

4. Divide dough in half. Shape the dough into two loaves about 10 inches long. Place on a parchment-lined cookie sheet, spacing them 3 inches apart.

5. Bake for 20 to 25 minutes, until tops of loaves are firm. Remove cookie sheet from the oven.

6. Using two metal spatulas, carefully remove loaves from hot cookie sheet onto wire racks. Cool. Place cooled loaves on cutting board. Using a sharp knife, cut the loaves diagonally into ½-inch-wide slices.

7. Place the slices on the cookie sheet in a single layer. Return to the oven for 12 to 15 minutes. Remove cookie sheet from the oven. Cool toasted biscotti on a wire cooling rack. Store cooled cookies in an airtight container.

YIELD: 24 BISCOTTI

LADY'S KISSES

BACI DI DAMA

These petite sandwich cookies are delicately flavored with an almond and chocolate filling. When using the pastry bag, try to make all the cookies the same size. This will make it easier to pair them with the filling.

COOKIE:

½ POUND BUTTER, SOFTENED

¾ CUP CONFECTIONERS' SUGAR

1 EGG

1 TEASPOON ALMOND EXTRACT

1½ CUPS FLOUR

PINCH OF SALT

FILLING:

½ CUP ALMONDS, FINELY GROUND

1 TABLESPOON ALMOND PASTE

1 CUP CHOCOLATE CHIPS

1. Preheat oven to 350°F.

2. In an electric mixer, cream the butter and confectioners' sugar. Add egg and almond extract. Mix well. On low speed, gradually add the flour and salt. Mix just until blended.

3. Using a pastry bag without a tip (coupler only), pipe 1-inch circles onto a parchment-lined cookie sheet, spacing cookies 2 inches apart.

4. Bake for 8 to 10 minutes, or until the edges of cookies begin to brown. Remove cookie sheet from the oven. Cool cookies on parchment.

5. Place almonds and almond paste in a food processor. Pulse until finely ground. Set aside.

6. Melt chocolate chips.

7. Using a butter knife, spread a thin layer of chocolate on the flat side of only 6 to 8 cookies at a time. Otherwise the chocolate will dry before you sandwich them. Dip

one chocolate side into almond mixture and press together with another flat sided cookie.

8. Repeat spreading and dipping in almond mixture until all cookies are matched.

YIELD: 30 COOKIES

♦ ALMOND PASTE ♦

THIS IS A POPULAR ITALIAN CONFECTION THAT IS MADE FROM AL-MONDS AND SUGAR. IT IS MASHED INTO A PASTE THAT IS USED FOR AMARETTI COOKIES. IT IS ALSO USED FOR MAKING MARZIPAN.

SICILIAN PISTACHIO BISCOTTI

These salty snacks are studded with pistachios. They're a great warm-weather snack or appetizer with a cold beer. Try to find pistachios that are already shelled. Whenever I buy pistachios in the shell, I barely have enough left after shelling. Suddenly everyone in the bakery wants to help shell them, just so they can sneak a few to munch on.

¼ POUND BUTTER, SOFTENED

¼ CUP SUGAR

1 TABLESPOON MARSALA WINE

2 EGGS

2 CUPS FLOUR

1½ CUPS COARSELY CHOPPED PISTA-CHIOS

1. Preheat oven to 350°F.

2. In an electric mixer, cream the butter and sugar. Add marsala and eggs. Mix until well blended. Add flour.

3. Roll dough into ¾-inch balls. Roll balls in water and then in pistachios to coat them. Place on a parchment-lined cookie sheet, spacing 2 inches apart. Flatten the tops slightly with your finger.

4. Bake for 20 to 25 minutes, or until golden brown.

5. Remove cookie sheet from the oven. Using a metal spatula, remove the cookies from the cookie sheet and place on a wire cooling rack. Cool. Store cookies in an airtight container.

YIELD: 24 COOKIES

VANILLA BISCOTTI

Using a vanilla bean to flavor these biscotti really gives it a rich natural taste. I love to wrap these cookies in small plastic bags and tie with festive ribbons. They are a great little make-ahead gift or shower favor.

1 CUP SUGAR	2 CUPS FLOUR
1 VANILLA BEAN	1 TEASPOON BAKING POWDER
¼ POUND BUTTER, SOFTENED	PINCH OF SALT
2 EGGS	

1. Preheat oven to 350°F.

2. Place sugar in a small bowl. Slice vanilla bean in half with a paring knife. Using the tip of the knife, scrape the vanilla into the sugar. Mix until well blended.

3. In an electric mixer, cream butter and vanilla sugar until light. Add eggs. Mix until well blended. On low speed, gradually add flour, baking powder, and salt.

4. Turn out dough onto a lightly floured surface. Divide dough in half. Roll each half into a cylinder about 12 inches long. Place cylinders on parchment-lined cookie sheet, spacing 3 inches apart.

5. Bake for 20 to 25 minutes, or until golden brown. Remove cookie sheet from the oven. Using two metal spatulas, carefully remove loaves from the cookie sheet and place on wire cooling racks. Cool. Place cooled loaves on a cutting board. Using a sharp knife, cut the loaves diagonally into ½-inch slices.

6. Place the slices on the cookie sheet in a single layer. Return to the oven for 12 to 15 minutes. Cool toasted biscotti on wire cooling rack. Store cooled cookies in an airtight container.

YIELD: 24 COOKIES

VENETIANS

*These bar cookies are a staple for most Italian bakeries. Their bright red, white, and
green colors will brighten up any cookie tray. The colors remind us of the Italian
flag or the vibrant colors of Murano glass in Venice.*

6 EGGS, SEPARATED	3 CUPS FLOUR
1½ CUPS SUGAR	¼ TEASPOON SALT
¼ TEASPOON CREAM OF TARTAR	2 CUPS APRICOT PRESERVES
1 POUND BUTTER, SOFTENED	2 CUPS SEMISWEET CHOCOLATE CHIPS
1 TEASPOON ALMOND EXTRACT	
12 OUNCES ALMOND PASTE	

1. Preheat oven to 350°F.

2. Grease and line three 15 x 10-inch cookie sheets, with sides, with parchment. Grease parchment. Set aside.

3. In an electric mixer with wire whisk, beat egg whites, ½ cup sugar, and cream of tartar until stiff, 2 to 3 minutes. Set aside.

4. In an electric mixer, cream the butter and remaining 1 cup of sugar. Add egg yolks and almond extract. Break up almond paste into small pieces. Add and mix until well blended and smooth. Add flour and salt. Mix until well blended.

5. With wire whisk attachment, fold in egg white mixture.

6. Divide dough into three equal portions. Add a few drops of red food coloring to one and a few drops of green coloring to another. Leave one dough natural color.

7. Evenly spread each dough into prepared pans. Each layer will be thin.

8. Bake each batter for 15 minutes or until the edges begin to brown. Remove pans from the oven.

9. Cool on wire cooling rack.

10. Remove and discard parchment. Place the green layer on a parchment-lined

cookie sheet. Spread one cup of apricot preserves over the green layer. Slide yellow layer of cake on top of the preserves. Spread remaining cup of preserves over yellow layer. Slide the red layer over the preserves. Cover with plastic wrap. Weigh down with a cutting board on top. Refrigerate overnight.

11. Melt 1 cup of chocolate chips. Spread in a thin layer over the top of the red layer. Let set until dry. Flip cake over onto parchment. Melt remaining cup of chocolate chips. Spread over green layer. Let set.

12. Using a serrated knife, trim edges. Cut into 1-inch squares.

YIELD: ABOUT 80 COOKIES

◆ BOMBONIERE ◆

ITALIAN BRIDAL SHOWERS AND WEDDINGS OFTEN FEATURE FAVORS COMPRISED OF SMALL BOXES OR BAGS FILLED WITH FANCY CANDIES OR COOKIES. A TRADITIONAL BOMBONIERA IS A SMALL CLUSTER OF CANDY-COATED ALMONDS WRAPPED IN TUILLE AND TIED WITH MONOGRAMMED RIBBON.

CHOCOLATE CALZONES

These chocolate- and walnut-filled pockets are deep-fried and delicious. Many people are familiar with calzones that use pizza dough to encase cheese and other toppings. This sweet calzone uses the same technique—a round piece of chocolate dough that encloses a delicious chocolate and nut filling.

DOUGH:

¼ POUND BUTTER, SOFTENED

¼ CUP COCOA

¼ CUP SOUR CREAM

¾ CUP FLOUR

FILLING:

¾ CUP CHOPPED WALNUTS

½ CUP SUGAR

VEGETABLE OIL FOR FRYING

½ CUP SEMISWEET CHOCOLATE CHIPS

¼ CUP HEAVY CREAM

1. In an electric mixer, cream butter until light. Add cocoa and sour cream. Mix until well blended. Add flour. Mix until just blended. Turn out dough onto a lightly floured surface. Knead until well blended. Wrap in plastic wrap and refrigerate for 2 to 3 hours or overnight.

2. In a medium saucepan, combine all filling ingredients. Heat on medium, stirring constantly until chocolate is melted. Set aside to cool.

3. Roll out dough on a lightly floured surface until ⅛ inch thick. Using a 3-inch-round cookie cutter or the rim of a juice glass, cut dough into circles. Place ½ teaspoon of filling in the center of each circle. Brush edges of circle with water. Fold dough over to form a turnover. Seal edges with a fork. Fill all the dough and let calzones rest for 15 to 20 minutes before frying.

4. Heat about 3 inches of vegetable oil over medium-high heat.

5. Deep-fry calzones in preheated oil until lightly browned. Remove from oil with a slotted spoon. Drain on absorbent paper. Dust with confectioners' sugar and serve warm or cool.

YIELD: 20 CALZONES

ITALIAN RING BISCUITS

CIAMBELLE

These slightly sweet ring-shaped taralle are perfect for breakfast, a snack,
or for appetizers. Be sure to bake them until they are golden brown
and they'll stay crunchy for days.

¼ CUP SUGAR	½ CUP WHITE WINE
½ CUP OIL	1¾ CUPS FLOUR

1. Preheat oven to 350°F.

2. In a medium mixing bowl, whisk together sugar, oil, and wine. Stir in flour. Turn out dough onto a lightly floured surface. Knead until well blended.

3. Roll dough into pencil-size pieces, about 5 inches long. Form into a ring and pinch ends together. Place on a parchment-lined cookie sheet, spacing each ring about 2 inches apart.

4. Bake for 25 to 30 minutes, or until golden brown.

5. Remove cookie sheet from the oven. Place cookies on wire cooling rack. Cool completely. Store unused ciambelle in plastic wrap at room temperature.

YIELD: 25 CIAMBELLE

ITALIAN LADYFINGERS

SAVOIARDI

These biscuits are thicker and crunchier than the ladyfingers most Americans know. They're hard on the outside yet spongy inside to absorb the espresso used to soak them while making tiramisù (see recipe page 141).

3 EGGS, SEPARATED	⅓ CUP FLOUR
½ TEASPOON CREAM OF TARTAR	½ CUP CORNSTARCH
8 TABLESPOONS SUGAR	4 TABLESPOONS WATER

1. Preheat oven to 350°F.

2. In an electric mixer with wire whisk attachment, whip egg whites and cream of tartar until stiff. Add 4 tablespoons of sugar. Whip until stiff. Set aside.

3. In an electric mixer, beat egg yolks and remaining 4 tablespoons sugar. Mix until light in color. Gradually add flour and cornstarch. Add water and mix until well blended.

4. Using a rubber spatula and small wrist-turning strokes, fold egg whites into yolk mixture. Batter will be light like a sponge cake batter. Spoon batter into a pastry bag without a tip. Pipe 5-inch strips onto a parchment-lined cookie sheet. You can pipe these cookies close together. If they spread while baking you can break apart after they cool.

5. Bake for 25 to 30 minutes, or until golden brown. Remove cookie sheet from the oven.

6. Cool cookies on parchment. When completely cool, carefully remove from parchment. Store unused cookies in a plastic bag at room temperature.

YIELD: 20 LADYFINGERS

APRICOT ORANGE BARS

*These bars are easy to make and look great on a cookie tray. Try cutting them into
squares, diamonds, or triangles. If you're stacking these cookies on a tray,
try to keep them on top so they won't crumble.*

CRUST:

¾ CUP FLOUR	½ CUP SUGAR
½ CUP SEMOLINA FLOUR	¼ POUND BUTTER, SOFTENED

FILLING:

1 CUP DRIED APRICOTS, CHOPPED	JUICE OF 1 ORANGE
GRATED RIND OF 1 ORANGE	1 CUP WATER

1. In a medium saucepan, combine all filling ingredients. Boil over low heat for 20 to 30 minutes, until apricots are tender and liquid is reduced. Set aside.

2. Preheat oven to 375°F.

3. Grease an 8-inch square cake pan. Set aside.

4. In a medium mixing bowl, combine flour, semolina flour, and sugar. Mix well. Using a pastry blender or two knives, cut butter into dry ingredients until mixture resembles coarse crumbs. Press half the crust mixture into the prepared pan. Spread filling on top of crust. Lightly press remaining crumb mixture evenly over the filling.

5. Bake for 30 to 35 minutes, or until lightly browned.

6. Remove pan from the oven. Place on wire cooling rack. Cool completely. Cut into 1-inch squares. Store unused cookies in an airtight container.

YIELD: 42 COOKIES

ALMOND BARS

These bars have a buttery crust topped with sliced almonds. Almonds are one of the most popular nuts used in Italian cooking. My mom and aunts fight to bring home from the bakery any extra toasted almonds to use in their string beans for dinner.

CRUST:

¾ CUP FLOUR	¼ POUND BUTTER, SOFTENED
¼ CUP SUGAR	

TOPPING:

2 EGGS	2 TABLESPOONS FLOUR
1 CUP SUGAR	1 TEASPOON BAKING POWDER
2 TABLESPOONS AMARETTO	1½ CUPS ALMONDS, SLICED

1. Preheat oven to 375°F.

2. Grease an 8-inch square cake pan. Set aside.

3. In a medium mixing bowl, combine flour and sugar. Using a pastry blender or two knives, cut butter into flour mixture until mixture resembles coarse crumbs. Press crumb mixture into prepared pan. Bake for 10 to 15 minutes, or until lightly browned.

4. Remove crust from the oven. Place on wire cooling rack. Prepare filling.

5. In another bowl, whisk eggs and sugar until thick. Blend in amaretto. Add flour, baking powder, and almonds. Mix until well blended.

6. Pour egg mixture on top of the prepared crust. Spread evenly.

7. Bake for 20 to 25 minutes, or until lightly browned.

8. Remove pan from the oven and place on wire cooling rack. Cool completely. Cut into 1-inch squares. Store unused cookies in an airtight container.

YIELD: 42 COOKIES

◆ A Taste of Italy ◆

One of my favorite times to visit Rome is around March 19, the feast day of Saint Joseph. One of my favorite pastry shops, near the Via Condotti, makes incredible zeppole di San Giuseppe, a delicious fried cruller filled with pastry cream. This is a fresh and fabulous treat that I can never re-create at home. Just before we were to leave for the airport on our most recent visit, my dad and I ran from the hotel to the pastry shop, just to have a final taste. I ordered, paid, and cradled my pretty package of three zeppole. I guess I didn't cradle the bundle well enough. In our mad dash back to the hotel, I heard a small thump and realized my precious package had slipped from my hands and onto the street. *O Dio!* My dad and I stared down in disbelief. We scooped them up, brought them back to the hotel room, and dusted off our zeppole. We salvaged a few small bites each. This was a real taste of Italy!

CAKES

Italian cakes are different from the ones that we make in America. They are generally more casual, single layer cakes that are richly flavored with nuts, fruits, and chocolate. Cakes are usually served plain, with a dusting of powdered sugar or with a dollop of whipped cream on top. There aren't many fussy frostings and elaborate decorations. Many of the fancier cakes, reserved for holidays, are sponge cakes with fresh fruit and a simple swirled sweetened whipped cream frosting. They are not like American layer cakes with fancy buttercream piping. Other cakes or tortes, as they are called, resemble what we would call a pie. However you classify them, they're delicious.

Mixing Tips

Start by having ingredients at room temperature. This is a vital point for cake baking. For butter-based cakes this insures that the butter blends easily with sugar and eggs. For foam-type cakes, like sponge cakes, room temperature egg whites will yield the most volume.

For cheesecakes, room temperature cheese and eggs are important for maximum volume.

Testing for Doneness

Many of these cakes are made of thick layers and require long baking times. These are great to prepare and put in the oven, then relax or do another task during the baking time. Use a cake tester, inserted into the center of the cake, to test for doneness. The tester should have a fine crumb, not batter, when removed. If you wait until the tester comes out clean, you might overbake the cake. Remember, the cake will continue to bake in the pan after it's removed.

Decorating

As I've previously mentioned, Italian cakes are more casual than American cakes. The decorating is so easy you may not even need a pastry bag. A simple dusting of confectioners' sugar or cocoa (for chocolate cakes) is enough for many of these rustic cakes. Dusting to form a pattern is easy and limited only by your creativity.

To make a diagonal pattern on a 9-inch cake:

Cut ½-inch-wide strips of baking parchment approximately 9 inches long. Place strips diagonally, ½ inch apart on top of cake. Place another set of parchment strips on the opposite diagonal, again about ½ inch apart. Be sure some of the cake is showing. Dust confectioners' sugar over the top. Carefully remove parchment strips to reveal design. You can use the same technique with a lace doily or any other type of stencil you choose.

Whipped Cream Frosted Cakes

Many of these sponge-based cakes use a stiff whipped cream frosting. Use a metal spatula to spread cream where desired. Use small swirled strokes to create a home-style look.

Covering Sides of Cakes with Nuts

An easy way to cover any frosting mistakes and create a professional-looking cake is to cover the cake with toasted nuts or coconut. Place nuts or coconut on a flat plate. Hold the cake from the bottom, with one hand. Use the other hand to press nuts or coconut onto the sides of the cake. Hold the cake over the plate to catch any excess that falls away.

Dusting with Confectioners' Sugar

To dust a cake or cake slice with confectioners' sugar, place a few tablespoons of powdered sugar in a small dry strainer. Hold the strainer over the cake and with a teaspoon stir the sugar over the cake in the desired amount.

SICILIAN CASSATA

There are many variations of this traditional Sicilian dessert, including a frozen version. Most Sicilian pastry shops have fancy marzipan-covered cassata with candied fruit. My favorite combination is still this classic pound cake filled with an orange ricotta filling and covered with a rich chocolate glaze. You can also serve this tasty, versatile cake with just a sprinkle of confectioners' sugar. Serve a generous slice with a cup of espresso for any special occasion.

POUND CAKE:

2 CUPS CAKE FLOUR	1½ STICKS BUTTER, SOFTENED
1 CUP SUGAR	3 EGGS
1 TEASPOON BAKING POWDER	¼ CUP MILK
PINCH OF SALT	

SWEET RICOTTA FILLING:

2 CUPS RICOTTA	GRATED RIND OF 1 ORANGE
½ CUP SUGAR	

CHOCOLATE GLAZE:

1½ CUPS SEMISWEET CHOCOLATE CHIPS	¼ POUND COLD BUTTER

1. Preheat oven to 350°F.

2. Grease and flour or line an 8 x 4-inch loaf pan with baking parchment. Set aside.

3. In an electric mixer, combine flour, sugar, baking powder, and salt. On low speed, add butter and mix until well blended. Add eggs and milk. Mix on medium speed until smooth, about 2 minutes.

4. Pour into prepared pan. Bake for 50 to 55 minutes, or until done.

5. Remove pan from the oven and place on a wire cooling rack. Let cool in pan for

10 minutes. Carefully remove cake from the pan and continue to cool on wire cooling rack. Remove and discard parchment. Cool completely before assembling cassata or wrap cake in plastic wrap. Store at room temperature overnight or freeze for later use.

6. In a small bowl, combine ricotta, sugar, and rind. Mix well with a wooden spoon. Refrigerate if not using immediately.

7. In a small saucepan, over low heat, stir chocolate chips with a wooden spoon until melted. Remove from the heat.

8. Stir in butter until smooth. Refrigerate to thicken glaze for frosting consistency.

9. To reheat, heat in a double boiler over simmering water.

10. Slice pound cake horizontally into 3 even layers. Place top layer cut side up on a serving plate or doily-covered cake circle.

11. Spread half the ricotta filling over cake, spreading to the edges. Place next layer of cake on top. Spread remaining filling on top of this layer. Top with last layer of cake.

12. Cover with plastic wrap and refrigerate until set, 2 to 3 hours or overnight. Do not attempt to frost when cassata is this fresh. It needs to be firm.

13. When cassata is set, use a metal spatula to spread chocolate glaze on top and sides of cassata. Garnish with candied orange rind. Refrigerate until serving. Serve chilled.

YIELD: ONE 3-LAYER 8 X 4 CAKE, ABOUT 12 SERVINGS

SPONGE CAKE

PANE DI SPAGNA

This classic sponge cake is the basis for many famous Italian desserts such as Zuppa Inglese and Neapolitan Cake. The key to this family classic is simple: beat your egg whites until firm and carefully fold into the yolk mixture for a light, fluffy, and fool-proof sponge. Baked in an ungreased tube pan, the cake will naturally cling to the sides and middle tube and will rise beautifully.

7 EGG WHITES, AT ROOM TEMPERATURE	7 EGG YOLKS
1½ CUPS SUGAR	1 TEASPOON VANILLA EXTRACT
½ TEASPOON CREAM OF TARTAR	1½ CUPS CAKE FLOUR
½ TEASPOON SALT	¼ CUP COLD WATER

1. Preheat oven to 325°F.

2. In an electric mixer with wire whisk attachment, beat egg whites, ¼ cup sugar, cream of tartar, and salt. Start on medium speed, then use high speed until very stiff peaks form, 3 to 4 minutes.

3. In a separate bowl, on medium speed, beat egg yolks, remaining 1¼ cups sugar, and vanilla. Beat until light in color, 2 to 3 minutes.

4. Add flour and water alternately to egg mixture. Start and end with the flour. Mix just until blended.

5. Using a rubber spatula, fold egg yolk mixture into whites. When blended, spoon batter into an ungreased 10-inch tube pan with removable bottom. Spread batter evenly.

6. Bake for 60 to 65 minutes, or until top is golden brown. Remove pan from the oven.

7. Invert tube pan to cool cake, about 1 hour.

8. When cool, carefully remove the cake from the pan. Use a sharp knife to loosen the outside of the cake from the sides of the pan.

YIELD: ONE 10-INCH CAKE, ABOUT 20 SLICES

NUT CAKE

TORTE DI NOCI

This cake is perfect for nut lovers and has a simple garnish of confectioners' sugar. Dust the entire surface of the cake or use strips of parchment to create an interesting design. For the cake itself, you can use any type of nut or any combination of nuts. Try my favorite, walnuts and hazelnuts.

3 EGGS	1 TEASPOON BAKING POWDER
2 CUPS SUGAR	1 CUP MILK
1 CUP OIL	½ CUP WALNUTS, FINELY CHOPPED
3 TEASPOONS AMARETTO OR OTHER NUT LIQUEUR	½ CUP HAZELNUTS, FINELY CHOPPED
2 CUPS CAKE FLOUR	

GLAZE:

½ CUP AMARETTO OR OTHER NUT LIQUEUR

1. Preheat oven to 350°F.

2. Grease and flour or line a 9 x 3-inch springform pan with baking parchment. Set aside.

3. In an electric mixer on medium-high speed, beat eggs. Gradually add sugar and beat until light in color and thick in texture. Add oil and liqueur. Beat until well blended.

4. In a small bowl, mix together flour and baking powder. Add the flour mixture alternately with the milk to the egg mixture, beginning and ending with the flour mixture.

5. Stir in walnuts and hazelnuts.

6. Pour batter into prepared pan. Bake for 1 hour and 35 to 40 minutes, or until done.

7. Remove from the oven. Cool cake in pan on wire cooling rack for 15 to 20 minutes. Remove cake from the pan. Using a long serrated knife, carefully cut the top of the cake to level it and remove a crust that will form during baking. Pour amaretto over cake. Turn cake upside down and finish cooling on wire rack. The bottom will become the flat top of the cake. Remove and discard parchment. Dust with confectioners' sugar or cocoa.

YIELD: ONE 9-INCH ROUND CAKE, ABOUT 15 SLICES

◆ ITALIAN DESSERTS ◆

ITALY IS A WORLD-CLASS SWEET MAKER. IN PART THIS IS BECAUSE OF ITS DIVERSITY. THE NORTHERN PART OF ITALY DRAWS FROM AUSTRIAN AND GERMAN STRUDEL MAKING AND TRADITIONAL FRENCH TART MAKING. SOUTHERN PORTIONS OF ITALY WERE INFLUENCED BY AFRICAN AND MIDDLE EASTERN CULTURES. IT IS THIS BLENDING OF CULTURES—COMBINED WITH CENTURIES OF ITS OWN TRADITION—THAT MAKES ITALY SUCH A RICH, UNIQUE CULTURE (WITH RICH, UNIQUE DESSERTS).

BLACK CAKE WITH CHESTNUT CREAM

TORTE DI NERO CON CREMA DI CASTAGNA

A rich flourless chocolate cake accented with a scoop of chestnut cream is my solution for satisfying chocolate lovers everywhere. This cake is amazingly versatile—try pairing it with an orange or raspberry sauce. It's so rich it can be served chilled, in slivers.

2 POUNDS SEMISWEET CHOCOLATE, CHOPPED

¼ POUND UNSALTED BUTTER

8 EGGS

CHESTNUT CREAM (SEE FOLLOWING RECIPE)

1. Preheat oven to 350°F.

2. Grease and line a 9 x 2-inch round cake pan with baking parchment. Set aside.

3. Over simmering water or in a double boiler, melt chocolate and butter over low heat. Remove from the heat.

4. Using an electric mixer, add eggs, two at a time, beating well after adding. Beat until smooth.

5. Pour into prepared pan. Place pan on a sheet cake pan. Carefully add water to the sheet pan. Place pans in oven and bake for 25 to 30 minutes, or until just firm in the center.

6. Remove from oven. Cool cake in pan on wire rack. Refrigerate 2 to 3 hours or overnight. Use a small paring knife to loosen the edges of the cake from the pan. Invert onto a plate and remove pan. Discard parchment.

7. Store cake in refrigerator until slicing. Pipe chestnut cream onto a slice of cake or spoon it over.

YIELD: ONE 9-INCH ROUND CAKE, ABOUT 25 SERVINGS

CHESTNUT CREAM
CREMA DI CASTAGNA

This chestnut cream is the perfect accent for our rich chocolate cake.
It also makes a perfect not too sweet dessert all on its own. Spoon into
a martini glass and top with a cherry.

1 CUP HEAVY CREAM

¼ CUP SUGAR

1 TABLESPOON DARK RUM

1 RECIPE CHESTNUT PURÉE (SEE FOL-
LOWING RECIPE), OR 8 OUNCES
CANNED PURÉE

1. In an electric mixer with wire whisk, beat heavy cream until soft peaks form. Add sugar and rum. Add chestnut purée (at room temperature).

2. Whip until stiff peaks form. Pipe onto a slice of cake to garnish or spoon onto slice and serve.

YIELD: ABOUT 2 CUPS

CHESTNUT PURÉE

Chestnut purée is hard to find in specialty shops, but you can make your own.
If you find it, substitute an 8-ounce can in the chestnut cream recipe.

1 POUND CHESTNUTS, SLIT

6 TABLESPOONS HEAVY CREAM

1. Place chestnuts in a medium saucepan. Cover with water and boil on medium high for 20 to 25 minutes. Remove pan from the stove. Drain.

2. Cool chestnuts slightly. Peel outer shell as well as the inner skin. If chestnuts break, that's OK.

3. Return shelled chestnuts to medium saucepan. Cover with water. Simmer over low heat until tender, 20 to 25 minutes. Drain.

4. Purée in a food processor until smooth, adding heavy cream. Let cool. At this point you can refrigerate the purée overnight in an airtight container and complete chestnut cream the next day.

POLENTA CAKE

This cornmeal cake is a variation of our classic sponge cake. To make the cornmeal extra fine, process for 2 minutes in a food processor. It's perfect on its own or as the basis for our Sour Cherry Cake (see following recipe).

7 EGG WHITES, AT ROOM TEMPERATURE	1 TEASPOON VANILLA EXTRACT
1¾ CUPS SUGAR	¾ CUP ALL-PURPOSE FLOUR
½ TEASPOON CREAM OF TARTAR	¾ CUP FINE YELLOW CORNMEAL
½ TEASPOON SALT	¼ CUP COLD WATER
7 EGG YOLKS	

1. Preheat oven to 325°F.

2. In an electric mixer with wire whisk attachment, beat egg whites, ¼ cup of sugar, cream of tartar, and salt. Start on medium speed, then use high speed until very stiff peaks form, 3 to 4 minutes.

3. In a separate bowl, with an electric mixer on medium speed, beat egg yolks, remaining 1½ cups sugar, and vanilla. Beat until light in color, 2 to 3 minutes.

4. In a small bowl, mix together flour and cornmeal. Add flour mixture and water alternately to egg mixture. Start and end with the flour mixture. Mix just until blended.

5. Using a rubber spatula, fold egg yolk mixture into egg whites. When blended, spoon batter into an ungreased 10-inch tube pan with removable bottom. Spread batter evenly.

6. Bake for 60 to 65 minutes, or until top is golden brown. Remove pan from the oven.

7. Invert tube pan to cool cake, about 1 hour.

8. When cool, carefully remove cake from the pan. Use a sharp knife to loosen the outside of the cake from the sides of the pan.

YIELD: ONE 10-INCH CAKE, ABOUT 20 SLICES

SOUR CHERRY CAKE

This rustic cake combines the interesting texture of our polenta cake with a rich sour cherry filling. These cherries really aren't sour, just a bit tart and not too sweet. The perfect complement to a fine Italian feast. Allow 15 to 20 minutes longer for double recipe of filling to become thickened.

1 RECIPE POLENTA CAKE (SEE PRE-
CEDING RECIPE)

1 RECIPE WHIPPED CREAM FROSTING
(SEE FOLLOWING RECIPE)

2 RECIPES SOUR CHERRY FILLING (SEE
PAGE 95)

1. Cut polenta cake horizontally into thirds. Place the bottom layer, top-side up, on a serving plate or doily-covered cake circle. Spread a thin layer of whipped cream frosting over the cake. Place half the cherry filling on top of the cream.

2. Place middle layer of cake on top of cherry filling. Repeat layering whipped cream, cherry filling, and cake. Reserve 3 teaspoons of filling to garnish the cake. Pour any excess juice from the cherry filling over the top of the cake to soak.

3. Using a metal spatula, frost the top and sides of the cake with whipped cream frosting. Dot the top with remaining cherry filling. Sprinkle with cocoa to garnish. Refrigerate until serving. Serve chilled.

YIELD: ONE 3-LAYER 10-INCH CAKE, ABOUT 25 SERVINGS

WHIPPED CREAM FROSTING

*This fresh, not-too-sweet frosting is the perfect way to frost
or garnish your baked goods.*

2 CUPS HEAVY CREAM   **½ CUP SUGAR**

In an electric mixer with wire whisk attachment, beat cream into peaks, 2 to 3 minutes. Add sugar and whip until stiff. Use immediately.

YIELD: 4 CUPS, ENOUGH TO FILL AND FROST A 3-LAYER 10-INCH CAKE

CAPRI CHOCOLATE CAKE

TORTE CAPRESE

This tasty cake originated on the Isle of Capri, one of my favorite spots in the world, home to the famous Blue Grotto. On a recent visit, I was in awe of this limestone cave that reflects the light to show an unbelievable shade of blue water. I was really afraid to get in the small rowboat to enter the grotto, but when I heard Giuseppe, our rower, singing "Volare," I knew everything would be fine.

8 EGGS, SEPARATED

¾ CUP SUGAR

¼ POUND BUTTER, SOFTENED

10 OUNCES SEMISWEET CHOCOLATE, MELTED

½ CUP FLOUR

1½ CUPS WALNUTS, FINELY CHOPPED

1. Preheat oven to 350°F.

2. Grease and line a 9 x 3-inch springform pan with baking parchment. Set aside.

3. In an electric mixer with wire whisk attachment, beat egg whites until stiff. Gradually add ¼ cup of sugar as you are beating. Set aside.

4. In electric mixer, on medium speed, cream the butter. Add remaining ½ cup sugar and beat until light. Add egg yolks, one at a time, beating well after adding each one. Add melted chocolate. Beat 2 minutes for a smooth batter, being sure to scrape the bottom and sides of the mixing bowl with a rubber spatula.

5. Stir in flour and walnuts.

6. Carefully fold egg whites into chocolate batter. Pour batter into prepared pan, smoothing the top evenly.

7. Bake for 1 hour and 15 to 20 minutes, or until done.

8. Remove cake from the oven and cool in pan on wire rack for 15 to 20 minutes. Remove cake from the pan. Use a long serrated knife to level off the top of the cake and remove a crust that may form during baking. Turn cake upside down.

Remove and discard parchment. Continue to cool cake on wire cooling rack. The bottom of the cake will become the flat top of the cake. Dust top with confectioners' sugar or cocoa and serve.

YIELD: ONE 9-INCH ROUND CAKE, ABOUT 20 SERVINGS

ITALIAN FRUITCAKE

TORTE DI FRUTTA SECCA

This fruitcake is one of my mom's Christmas specialties. Her original recipe used milk, which I've replaced with a generous amount of sour cream. This adds a nice flavor and moisture to the cake. This recipe yields three small loaf cakes, making it a perfect gift for yourself and two of your friends.

½ POUND BUTTER, SOFTENED

2 CUPS SUGAR

4 EGGS

2 TABLESPOONS MARSALA

3 CUPS CAKE FLOUR

1 TEASPOON BAKING SODA

1½ CUPS SOUR CREAM

GRATED RIND OF 1 ORANGE

GRATED RIND OF 1 LEMON

1 CUP GLACÉ CHERRIES, HALVED

1 CUP DRIED APRICOTS, COARSELY CHOPPED

2 CUPS WALNUTS, COARSELY CHOPPED

SOAKING GLAZE:

½ CUP MARSALA

JUICE OF 1 LEMON

JUICE OF 1 ORANGE

1. Preheat oven to 350°F.

2. Grease and line 3 small loaf pans (about 7 x 3 inches) with baking parchment. Set aside.

3. In an electric mixer, cream butter and sugar until light. Add eggs, one at a time, beating well after adding each one. Add marsala. Mix until well blended.

4. In a small bowl, mix flour with baking soda. Add flour mixture to the egg mixture alternately with the sour cream. Begin and end with the flour mixture. Mix just until blended. Stir in orange and lemon rinds, cherries, apricots, and nuts.

5. Spoon batter evenly into prepared pans. Bake for 60 to 70 minutes, or until done. Remove cakes from the oven and place on wire cooling rack.

6. In a small bowl, mix marsala with lemon and orange juice. Pour evenly over hot

cakes. Continue to cool on wire cooling racks. Dust with confectioners' sugar and serve. Store unused cakes in foil or plastic wrap at room temperature for 1 week. For longer storage, freeze.

YIELD: THREE 7 X 3-INCH LOAVES, ABOUT 12 SLICES

ESPRESSO CHEESECAKE

This creamy cheesecake has the subtle flavor of coffee. Serve it with the espresso topping
or with fresh fruit. People often ask me how to prevent cheesecakes from cracking.
There are many causes for the cracking, which usually occurs during the cooling process.
Try to cool the cake gradually by leaving it in the warm oven after baking.
If it still cracks, just use a generous amount of topping.

CRUST:

1 CUP GRAHAM CRACKER CRUMBS	½ CUP SUGAR
4 TABLESPOONS COCOA	¼ POUND BUTTER, MELTED

FILLING:

2 POUNDS CREAM CHEESE, SOFTENED	4 EGGS, SLIGHTLY BEATEN
1 CUP SUGAR	1 CUP SOUR CREAM
4 TEASPOONS INSTANT ESPRESSO POWDER	

1. Preheat oven to 350°F.

2. Grease and line the sides of a 9 x 3-inch springform pan with baking parchment.

3. In a small bowl, combine graham cracker crumbs, cocoa, and sugar. Mix until blended. Add melted butter and mix with your fingers.

4. Press crust into the bottom of the pan. Bake for 5 minutes, or until set. Remove from the oven. Set aside to cool on a wire cooling rack.

5. In an electric mixer on medium-high speed, beat cream cheese until light and fluffy, about 15 minutes. Gradually add sugar and instant espresso. Mix until smooth and well blended. Add eggs gradually, beating well until blended. Stir in sour cream on low speed and mix just until blended.

6. Pour batter into prepared crust. Bake for 1 hour and 20 to 25 minutes, until center is just about set. Turn off oven. Let cake cool in oven for 15 to 20 minutes.

7. Remove cake from the oven and continue to cool on wire cooling rack. When completely cool, cover top of cake with plastic wrap or foil and refrigerate overnight.

8. To remove cake from pan, use a sharp straight knife. Run the edge of the knife along the outside of the cake. Pop open spring on springform pan.

9. Frost with coffee topping (see following recipe) and refrigerate until serving. Serve chilled.

YIELD: ONE 9-INCH CAKE, ABOUT 20 SERVINGS

COFFEE TOPPING

16 OUNCES CREAM CHEESE, SOFTENED   1 TABLESPOON COFFEE LIQUEUR

2 TEASPOONS INSTANT ESPRESSO   ½ CUP CONFECTIONERS' SUGAR

In an electric mixer on high speed, beat the cream cheese until fluffy, 4 to 5 minutes. Add instant espresso, coffee liqueur, and confectioners' sugar. Mix until well blended. Using a metal spatula, spread topping on top of cheesecake in a swirling pattern.

AUNT GIULIA'S ORANGE CAKE
TORTE D'ARANCIA

This is another of my aunt Giulia's specialties. It's a delicious pound cake, perfect served plain or with a dollop of ice cream or whipped cream. Not only was Aunt Giulia a great baker, but her basement served as our family party headquarters. It was fully equipped with a kitchen, player piano, and Ping-Pong table that doubled as our buffet table. The perfect place for birthday parties, showers, and family reunions. A lot of memories—and great cakes—were made there.

4 EGGS, SEPARATED	2½ CUPS CAKE FLOUR
½ POUND BUTTER, SOFTENED	PINCH OF SALT
2 CUPS SUGAR	2 TEASPOONS BAKING POWDER
GRATED RIND FROM 1 ORANGE	1 CUP ORANGE JUICE

1. Preheat oven to 350°F.

2. Grease and flour or line a 9 x 3-inch springform pan with baking parchment. Set aside.

3. In an electric mixer, with wire whisk attachment, beat egg whites until stiff. Set aside.

4. With electric mixer, cream butter until fluffy. Add sugar and orange rind. Add egg yolks, one at a time, beating well after adding each one.

5. In a separate bowl, combine flour, salt, and baking powder. Add the flour mixture to the butter mixture alternately with the orange juice, beginning and ending with the flour mixture.

6. Carefully fold egg whites into the flour mixture. Place batter into prepared pan.

7. Bake for 1 hour and 35 to 40 minutes, or until done.

8. Remove pan from the oven. Place cake on cooling rack and cool for 15 to 20 minutes. Carefully remove cake from the pan. Remove and discard parchment. Use a

long serrated knife to level off the top of cake and remove crust that may form during baking. Turn cake upside down. The flat bottom of the cake will become your level top. Continue to cool on wire cooling rack. Serve at room temperature. Dust top with confectioners' sugar.

YIELD: ONE 9-INCH CAKE, ABOUT 20 SLICES

ITALIAN CHEESECAKE

This ricotta cheesecake can be served plain, topped with fresh fruit or a rich chocolate sauce. I've given this traditional recipe a nutty graham cracker crust that's one of my favorites. It's easy to make and complements the creamy cake perfectly.

NUT CRUST:

1 CUP GRAHAM CRACKER CRUMBS	½ CUP WALNUTS, FINELY CHOPPED
½ CUP SUGAR	¼ POUND BUTTER, MELTED

FILLING:

4 CUPS RICOTTA	¼ CUP FLOUR
½ CUP SUGAR	4 TABLESPOONS AMARETTO
4 EGGS	¼ CUP HEAVY CREAM

1. Preheat oven to 325°F.

2. Grease and line the sides of a 9 x 3-inch springform pan with baking parchment.

3. In a small bowl, combine graham cracker crumbs, sugar, and nuts. Stir until blended. Add melted butter and mix with your fingers. Press crust mixture into the bottom of the prepared pan. Bake for 5 to 8 minutes, or until set. Remove from the oven and set aside to cool on a wire cooling rack.

4. In an electric mixer on medium speed, blend ricotta and sugar. Add eggs and beat until well blended. Add flour, amaretto, and heavy cream. Mix just until blended. Pour batter into prepared crust.

5. Bake for 1 hour and 20 to 25 minutes, until center is just set. Turn off oven. Let cake cool in oven for 15 to 20 minutes. Remove cake from the oven. Continue to cool cake on wire cooling rack. Wrap cake in plastic or foil. Refrigerate overnight.

6. To remove cake from the pan, use a straight knife. Run the edge of the knife

around the outside of the cake. Pop open the spring on the springform pan to re-lease cake. Dust with confectioners' sugar or top with fresh fruit. Refrigerate until serving. Serve chilled.

YIELD: ONE 9-INCH CHEESECAKE, ABOUT 20 SERVINGS

TUSCAN HARVEST CAKE

TORTE DI TOSCANO

This crumb cake is perfect for breakfast or to take along on a picnic. When grinding almonds in a food processor, add a teaspoon or two of sugar. This will help absorb the oils that are released when chopping nuts. These oils can make the nuts too moist for most recipes.

2 CUPS DICED APPLES (ABOUT 2 APPLES)

2 CUPS SUGAR

GRATED RIND OF 1 LEMON

JUICE OF 1 LEMON

1 TEASPOON CINNAMON

½ POUND BUTTER, SOFTENED

2 EGGS

1 TEASPOON VANILLA

1½ CUPS FLOUR

1 CUP GROUND ALMONDS

1. Preheat oven to 375°F.

2. Grease and flour or line a 9-inch round cake pan with baking parchment. Set aside.

3. In a medium bowl, combine apples, 1 cup of sugar, lemon rind and juice, and cinnamon. With a wooden spoon, mix until well blended. Set aside.

4. In an electric mixer, cream butter and remaining 1 cup of sugar until light. Add eggs and vanilla. Mix until well blended. On low speed, gradually add flour and chopped almonds. Mix just until blended.

5. Spread dough into prepared pan. Spread apple mixture evenly over the top of the dough.

6. Bake for 40 to 45 minutes, or until done in the center.

7. Remove pan from the oven. Place on wire cooling rack. Cool. Cut into wedges and serve warm or completely cool.

YIELD: ONE 9-INCH CAKE, ABOUT 12 SERVINGS

ENGLISH TRIFLE WITH STRAWBERRIES AND MARSALA
ZUPPA INGLESE CON FRAGOLE E MARSALA

A traditional zuppa inglese is an English Trifle with sponge cake, custard, and whipped cream. My updated variation adds fresh strawberries and a hint of marsala wine— delizioso! You'll need a trifle bowl, which looks like a large square brandy snifter, to assemble this dessert. Make your own variations using a different type of wine, liqueur, or fresh fruit.

1 RECIPE SPONGE CAKE (SEE PAGE 46)

½ CUP MARSALA WINE

1 RECIPE VANILLA PASTRY CREAM (SEE PAGE 95)

16 OUNCES STRAWBERRIES, CLEANED, HULLED, AND SLICED

¾ CUP HEAVY CREAM

2 TABLESPOONS SUGAR

1. Cut sponge cake horizontally into thirds. Place the bottom layer, cut side up, in the bottom of the trifle bowl. Using a pastry brush, brush all the layers of sponge evenly with the marsala.

2. Spread half of the pastry cream over the bottom layer of sponge cake. Arrange half the strawberries around the bowl and covering the custard. Place the middle layer of sponge on top of the strawberries. Spread remaining half of pastry cream and strawberries on the middle sponge cake. Top with final layer. Lightly press all the cake down in the bowl.

3. In an electric mixer on high speed, beat heavy cream until stiff. Add sugar and beat until well blended. Spoon dollops or pipe dollops from a pastry bag on top of the trifle. Dust the entire top with confectioners' sugar. Place whole strawberries in the center of the dollop. Refrigerate until serving. Serve chilled.

YIELD: ABOUT 25 SERVINGS

NEAPOLITAN CAKE

This cake is based on the Neapolitan pastry that layers sponge cake with phyllo pastry, fresh fruit, and whipped cream. The result is a light cake with a crunchy surprise layer of baked phyllo.

6 SHEETS OF COMMERCIAL PHYLLO DOUGH, THAWED

2 TABLESPOONS BUTTER, SOFTENED

½ RECIPE SPONGE CAKE

½ RECIPE WHIPPED CREAM FROSTING (SEE PAGE 54)

3 CUPS SLICED STRAWBERRIES AND WHOLE RASPBERRIES

1. Preheat oven to 375°F.

2. Brush each sheet of phyllo with soft butter and layer all 6 layers.

3. Using a sharp straight knife, cut a 9-inch circle from the dough. Place on parchment-lined cookie sheet. Bake for 10 to 15 minutes, or until golden. Cool on parchment.

4. Carefully slice the sponge cake horizontally in half. Place the bottom layer, cut side up, on a serving plate or doily-covered cake circle. Spread a thin layer of whipped cream frosting over the cake. Spread half the berry mixture over the cream. Place phyllo circle on top of the berries. Spread a thin layer of whipped cream on the phyllo circle. Top with layer of sponge cake. Spread layer of cream, and remaining berries, on top.

5. Dust with confectioners' sugar. Refrigerate until serving. Serve chilled.

YIELD: ONE 3-LAYER 10-INCH CAKE, ABOUT 25 SERVINGS

TO MAKE HALF THE SPONGE CAKE

4 EGG WHITES	4 EGG YOLKS
2 TABLESPOONS PLUS ½ CUP SUGAR	½ TEASPOON VANILLA EXTRACT
¼ TEASPOON CREAM OF TARTAR	¾ CUP CAKE FLOUR
¼ TEASPOON SALT	2 TABLESPOONS COLD WATER

1. Preheat oven to 325°F.

2. In an electric mixer with wire whisk attachment, beat egg whites, 2 tablespoons of sugar, cream of tartar, and salt. Start on medium speed, then use high speed until very stiff peaks form, 3 to 4 minutes. Set aside.

3. In a separate bowl, with an electric mixer on medium speed, beat the egg yolks, ½ cup sugar, and vanilla. Beat until light in color, 2 to 3 minutes.

4. Alternate adding flour and water to egg yolk mixture. Begin and end with the flour. Mix just until well blended.

5. Using a rubber spatula, fold egg yolk mixture into beaten whites. When blended, spoon batter into a 10-inch ungreased tube pan with removable bottom.

6. Bake for 30 minutes, or until top is golden brown. Remove pan from the oven. Invert cake and cool in pan for about 1 hour.

7. When cool, carefully remove the cake from the pan. Use a sharp straight knife to loosen the outside of the cake from the pan. Remove inside of pan. Run knife along the bottom and around inside of center column to remove.

THOUSAND-LAYER APRICOT CAKE
MILLEFOGLIE

*This cake is really more like a giant pastry. It is simple to make,
impressive to serve, and light to eat. Millefoglie literally means many leaves,
referring to the many layers of the pastry.*

1 BOX FROZEN PUFF PASTRY

1 RECIPE APRICOT CREAM (SEE FOL-
LOWING RECIPE)

1. Preheat oven to 400°F.

2. Thaw 2 sheets of puff pastry according to the directions on the box. On a lightly
floured surface, roll puff pastry as thin as possible into a rectangle about 9 x 7
inches. Using a sharp straight knife, cut sheet in half so that each piece measures
about 4½ x 7 inches. Prick each sheet with a fork several times. Place sheets on a
parchment-lined cookie sheet, spacing each sheet about 1 inch apart.

3. Repeat rolling and cutting the second sheet, same as the first. Bake for 15 to 18
minutes, or until well browned.

4. Remove pan from the oven. Cool dough on parchment on wire cooling rack.
Wrap in plastic and store at room temperature overnight, if desired, or assemble
when cool.

5. Place a piece of baked puff pastry, top side up, on a serving plate or doily-covered
cake circle. Using a metal spatula, spread one third of the apricot cream evenly on
pastry. Place another sheet on top of apricot cream. Repeat layering another one
third of apricot cream and another layer of pastry until plain pastry is at the top.

6. Dust top with confectioners' sugar. Refrigerate until serving. Serve chilled.

YIELD: ONE 4 X 7-INCH CAKE, ABOUT 8 SLICES

APRICOT CREAM

This cream can be used as a filling for the Millefoglie, a sponge cake, or simply spooned into a cup and enjoyed on its own.

1½ CUPS HEAVY CREAM

½ CUP SUGAR

½ CUP APRICOT PIE FILLING OR PRE-SERVES

In an electric mixer with wire whisk attachment, beat heavy cream until thick. Add sugar and beat on high speed until stiff. Add apricot pie filling. Mix until well blended. Use immediately.

AMARETTO CHIFFON CAKE

*This light, flavorful cake has a rich almond taste. The key to this cake is to beat
your egg whites until very stiff, which will produce the most volume and
a light and fluffy cake. Serve with a dusting of confectioners' sugar, a dollop of
whipped cream, and fresh fruit.*

6 EGGS, SEPARATED	2¼ CUPS FLOUR
½ TEASPOON CREAM OF TARTAR	3 TEASPOONS BAKING POWDER
1¼ CUPS SUGAR	¾ CUP AMARETTO
½ CUP VEGETABLE OIL	

1. Preheat oven to 325°F.

2. In an electric mixer with wire whisk attachment, beat egg whites, cream of tartar,
   and ½ cup of sugar. Beat on high until stiff peaks form. Set aside.

3. In an electric mixer on medium speed, beat egg yolks. Gradually add remaining
   sugar and oil. Beat until light in color.

4. In a small bowl, combine flour and baking powder. Add the flour mixture alternately with the amaretto to the egg yolk mixture. Begin and end with the flour
   mixture.

5. Using a rubber spatula, carefully fold egg whites into flour mixture. Pour batter
   into an ungreased 10-inch tube pan with a removable bottom.

6. Bake for 50 to 55 minutes. Remove cake from the oven. Invert cake to cool. Cool
   completely. Use a sharp knife to loosen cake from around the sides and bottom of
   the pan. Dust with confectioners' sugar and serve.

YIELD: ONE 10-INCH CAKE, ABOUT 20 SERVINGS

MANDARIN ORANGE
MERINGUE CAKE

These striking cakes are all over the pastry shops of Italy. The light sponge and chocolate pastry cream is hidden by a covering of meringues and mandarin oranges. Fill and frost the cake first and then arrange baked meringues and mandarin oranges into whipped cream, covering the entire outer surface.

½ RECIPE SPONGE CAKE (SEE PAGE 46)

1 RECIPE CHOCOLATE PASTRY CREAM
(SEE FOLLOWING RECIPE)

1 CUP HEAVY CREAM

¼ CUP SUGAR

1 RECIPE COCOA ALMOND MERINGUES
(SEE PAGE 68)

1 CUP MANDARIN ORANGES

1. Carefully cut sponge cake horizontally into thirds. Place the bottom layer, cut side up, on a serving dish or doily-covered cake circle. Spread half the chocolate pastry cream over the cake. Place the middle layer of sponge on top of the pastry cream. Spread remaining pastry cream over middle layer, and place remaining layer on top. Refrigerate cake while making the whipped cream frosting.

2. In an electric mixer on high speed, beat heavy cream until peaks begin to form. Add sugar and beat until stiff.

3. Using a metal spatula, frost the top and sides of the cake with whipped cream. Don't worry if you have crumbs in your frosting because you're going to cover the cake completely with the meringues.

4. While the frosting is fresh, place meringues and mandarin oranges all over the top and sides of the cake. Place flat side of meringue onto surface of the cake. Refrigerate overnight. Serve chilled.

YIELD: ONE 3-LAYER CAKE, ABOUT 20 SERVINGS

CHOCOLATE PASTRY CREAM

Use this cream to fill cake layers, cream puffs, or cannoli.

3 EGG YOLKS

½ CUP SUGAR

1½ CUPS MILK

1 TEASPOON VANILLA

2 TEASPOONS CORNSTARCH

1 TABLESPOON FLOUR

¼ CUP COCOA

1. In a medium mixing bowl or the top of a double boiler, whisk egg yolks and sugar until light. Add milk, vanilla, cornstarch, flour, and cocoa. Whisk over boiling water until thickened, 15 to 20 minutes.

2. Cool to room temperature. Cover with plastic wrap and refrigerate until using.

PIES AND TARTS

◆ ◆ ◆

Italian pies are usually baked in a deep pie dish, with a top crust or without. Tarts are made in shallow-sided pans, usually with removable bottoms to lift the tart out of the pan. They both use similar dough for crusts.

Tips on Making Crust

Most of the pies and tarts in this chapter use a tender dough, or *pasta frolla*. There are many variations of this dough. The master recipe I've included is a rich buttery version.

There are two easy methods to make pie crust dough. You can use either a food processor or a pastry blender to blend cold butter into the flour, or you can use two knives to cut the butter in. This mixture should resemble coarse crumbs. Then add your wet ingredients and knead until blended. Remember to begin with cold butter and cold water. This will give you the flakiest and most flavorful crusts.

For easiest rolling, refrigerate the dough before rolling. To roll, use a rolling pin on a lightly floured surface. You may need to lightly dust the rolling pin as well. (Be sure not to overflour the surface or the rolling pin, which will toughen the dough.) Keep moving the dough as you roll it out to be sure it's not sticking. Roll evenly from the inside out. Do not turn the dough over while rolling. Keep rolling the same side. The crust should be rolled about 1 inch larger than the pan it will fit. This will give you ample room for the sides.

To Make Lattice Top

Roll out dough as thin as the bottom crust, about ⅛ inch thick. Use a fluted pastry cutter to cut strips about ½ inch wide. Carefully lay strips horizontally over the top of the pie, spacing about ½ inch apart. Repeat laying strips ½ inch apart vertically to form lattice. Pinch ends of strips to bottom crust to adhere.

Prebaking a Bottom Crust

For some tart recipes you must bake the bottom crust empty, then cool and fill with filling. Because the tart is empty, there is nothing to hold the crust securely in place. You can use specially made pie weights, available in most kitchen shops, or the old-fashioned way of using dried beans as weights.

Fill the tart pan with bottom crust. Place a small piece of foil on the bottom. Place pie weights or beans on top of the foil. Bake as recipe directs. When cool, remove weights or beans.

You can also partially bake the bottom crust for some of these tarts, to avoid soggy bottoms.

TENDER PIE DOUGH

PASTA FROLLA

Pasta frolla means "tender dough" and is the basis for many of the sweet pies and tarts in this chapter. It is very versatile, buttery, and easy to work with. It freezes easily, so if you need to make just half the recipe, such as for a lemon or fig tart, just wrap the unused dough in plastic wrap and freeze. You can also use any extra dough to make pasta frolla cookies. This will give you two different desserts with only one dough to mix.

2 CUPS FLOUR	1½ STICKS BUTTER, CHILLED
⅔ CUP SUGAR	1 EGG
PINCH OF SALT	2 TABLESPOONS COLD WATER

1. Combine flour, sugar, and salt in a food processor. Pulse in butter until well blended into dry ingredients.

2. Add egg and water and pulse until blended.

3. Turn out dough onto a lightly floured surface and knead until well blended.

4. Separate dough in half. Wrap each in plastic and refrigerate from 2 to 3 hours or overnight.

YIELD: TWO 9-INCH TART OR PIE CRUSTS

PIE CRUST, OR PASTA FROLLA, COOKIES

These cookies started out as a great way to use any extra pie dough, but they've become popular in their own right, and now I sometimes make pasta frolla just to make them. The dough is rolled out, spread with a very thin layer of jelly, rolled like a jelly roll, and cut into slices.

PASTA FROLLA (SEE PRECEDING RECIPE)   JELLY, ANY FLAVOR

1. Preheat oven to 375°F.

2. Roll out dough on a lightly floured surface into a rectangular shape, about ⅛ inch thick. Using a metal spatula, spread a very thin layer of jelly over the dough. Carefully roll the dough, jelly roll fashion, beginning at the long portion. Roll into cylinder.

3. Place cylinders on parchment-lined cookie sheet. Cover with plastic wrap. Refrigerate 2 to 3 hours or overnight.

4. Cut into ½-inch slices. Place slices cut side up on a parchment-lined cookie sheet.

5. Bake for 20 to 25 minutes, or until lightly browned.

6. Remove cookie sheet from the oven. Use a metal spatula to remove cookies from the cookie sheet and place onto a wire cooling rack. Cool completely.

YIELD: WILL VARY ACCORDING TO HOW MUCH DOUGH YOU ARE USING

LEMON TART

CROSTATA DI LIMONE

A perfect after-dinner treat for any meal, this tart has the fresh taste of lemons that are
so popular throughout southern Italy. Because lemons are available in North America
year-round, this tart makes both a perfect refreshing summer dessert
and a great winter treat.

½ RECIPE PASTA FROLLA (SEE PAGE 78)   5 TABLESPOONS BUTTER, MELTED

¾ CUP SUGAR   JUICE AND RIND OF 2 LEMONS (⅓ CUP)

2 EGGS

1. Make pasta frolla. Chill for 2 to 3 hours or overnight.

2. Preheat oven to 350°F.

3. Roll out dough on a lightly floured surface until ⅛ inch thick. Carefully line the
   bottom of a 9-inch tart pan with removable bottom with dough. Roll your rolling
   pin over top of pan to cut dough. Partially cook crust with pie weights 15 minutes.
   Remove from oven. Cool completely.

4. In an electric mixer, beat sugar and eggs. Add cooled butter and lemon rind and
   juice. Pour lemon mixture into prepared crust.

5. Bake for 30 minutes, or until filling is set and crust is golden brown.

6. Remove from the oven. Place tart on wire cooling rack. Cool completely. Refrigerate overnight.

7. Carefully remove tart from pan. Refrigerate until serving. Serve chilled. Dust
   with confectioners' sugar and serve with fresh fruit.

YIELD: ONE 9-INCH TART, ABOUT 8 SERVINGS

FRESH FIG TART
CROSTATA DI FICO

This fresh fig tart is one of my mom's favorite desserts. It reminds me of late summer when figs are in season and plentiful in Italy. It's a perfect dessert to enjoy with coffee at an outdoor café, or on your own porch. I am happily continuing my family's summer ritual of having espresso al fresco every night, weather permitting, and this tart makes it perfect.

½ RECIPE PASTA FROLLA (SEE PAGE 78)

2 EGG YOLKS

½ CUP SUGAR

1 CUP MILK

3 TABLESPOONS FLOUR

3 TABLESPOONS RUM

6 FRESH FIGS, BLACK OR GREEN, CUT INTO THIN SLICES

½ CUP HAZELNUTS, CHOPPED

1. Preheat oven to 350°F.

2. Roll out chilled dough on a lightly floured surface until ⅛ inch thick. Carefully place crust in bottom of 9-inch tart pan with removable bottom. Add pie weights or beans and bake crust for 15 to 20 minutes. Remove crust from the oven. Cool on wire cooling rack.

3. In an electric mixer or with a wire whisk in medium bowl, beat egg yolks and sugar until light. Add milk, flour, and rum. Mix until well blended and smooth. Pour filling into cooled crust.

4. Arrange sliced figs around filling. Sprinkle figs with chopped hazelnuts.

5. Bake for 30 to 35 minutes, or until center is set. Remove from the oven. Cool tart on wire cooling rack. Refrigerate until serving. Serve chilled.

YIELD: ONE 9-INCH TART, ABOUT 8 SERVINGS

FRUIT TART

CROSTATA DI FRUTTA

This versatile tart has a rich pastry cream topped with any type of fresh fruit. I like to arrange the fruit on top in casual clusters rather than the classic concentric circle or structured arrangement. The crumbs that are sprinkled on the base of this tart are a great way to use less-than-fresh amaretti cookies. Another example of Italian recycling!

½ RECIPE PASTA FROLLA (SEE PAGE 78)

½ RECIPE PASTRY CREAM (SEE FOL-
LOWING RECIPE)

½ CUP CRUSHED AMARETTI COOKIES
(ABOUT 4 COOKIES CHOPPED IN FOOD
PROCESSOR)

ABOUT 4 CUPS MIXED FRUIT (SLICED
STRAWBERRIES, KIWI, BLUEBERRIES,
GRAPES)

1. Preheat oven to 350°F.

2. Roll out pasta frolla on a lightly floured surface until ⅛ inch thick. Place in bottom of 9-inch tart pan. Press into pan. Roll your rolling pin over the top of the pan to cut dough. Save any dough scraps. You can store in freezer and later make cookies (see page 79).

3. Sprinkle chopped amaretti cookies over crust.

4. Bake for 20 to 25 minutes, or until crust is lightly browned. Remove from the oven and cool on wire cooling rack.

5. Carefully remove cooled tart shell from the pan. Place on serving dish. Spread cooled pastry cream into baked tart shell. Arrange fruit slices on pastry cream. Sprinkle with 1 tablespoon additional sugar. Cover with plastic wrap and refrigerate until serving. Serve chilled.

YIELD: ONE 9-INCH TART, ABOUT 6 SERVINGS

PASTRY CREAM

This basic custard is so flexible it is an ideal filling for tarts, cakes, and cream puffs.

2 TEASPOONS CORNSTARCH

½ CUP SUGAR

3 EGG YOLKS

1½ CUPS MILK

½ TEASPOON VANILLA

1. In a mixing bowl over water or double boiler over medium heat, whisk cornstarch, sugar, egg yolks, and milk. Whisk constantly over boiling water until thick, about 20 minutes.

2. Remove from the heat. Stir in vanilla. Let cool before filling tart. Can be prepared 1 day ahead. Just cover and refrigerate.

CHRISTMAS TART
CROSTATA DI NATALE

A vivid red cranberry tart studded with walnuts and finished with a lattice top is a fancy and delicious addition to your holiday dessert table. To make the lattice, use a fluted pastry cutter for a pretty edge. I still have my aunt Giulia's cutter that her brother handcrafted for her in our local factory. It's a large fluted wheel that has had a lot of experience cutting pastry.

1 RECIPE PASTA FROLLA (SEE PAGE 78)	JUICE AND RIND OF 1 LEMON
I CUP SUGAR	1 CUP LARGE WALNUT PIECES
1 TABLESPOON CORNSTARCH	4 CUPS CRANBERRIES
¼ CUP WATER	4 TABLESPOONS BUTTER
½ CUP CORN SYRUP	

1. In a medium saucepan, combine sugar, cornstarch, water, corn syrup, and juice and rind of lemon. Heat over medium heat until boiling. Add walnuts and cranberries. Cook until cranberries pop, about 4 minutes.

2. Remove from the heat. Stir in butter. Let cool.

3. Preheat oven to 350°F.

4. Roll out chilled pasta frolla on a lightly floured surface until about ⅛ inch thick. Line the bottom of a 9-inch tart pan with half of the dough. Pour cooled cranberry filling into crust.

5. Use a fluted pastry cutter to cut ½-inch strips of remaining dough. Arrange strips in lattice fashion on top of the filling. Pinch edges to seal top lattice crust to bottom crust.

6. Bake for 35 to 40 minutes, or until crust is golden brown.

7. Remove tart from the oven. Let cool on wire cooling rack. When completely cool, remove tart from pan.

8. Serve plain or with ice cream or whipped cream.

YIELD: ONE 9-INCH TART, ABOUT 12 SERVINGS

PEAR AND PINE NUT TART

This pear and pine nut combination is a simple rustic treat. Because we had a pear tree in our backyard we always had a bumper crop, and my mom was always looking for desserts to use pears. My brother and I would pick the pears, divide them into portions in brown bags, and use our wagon to distribute to family and neighbors.

½ RECIPE PASTA FROLLA (SEE PAGE 78)

½ CUP PINE NUTS

3 EGGS

1 CUP SUGAR

1 TABLESPOON CORNSTARCH

1 CUP SOUR CREAM

GRATED RIND OF 1 LEMON

½ CUP HEAVY CREAM

4 RIPE PEARS, PEELED, CORED, AND CUBED

1. Preheat oven to 400°F.

2. Grease the bottom and line the sides of a 9 x 3-inch springform pan with baking parchment.

3. Using your fingers, press pasta frolla evenly into the bottom of prepared pan. Sprinkle with ¼ cup of pine nuts. Bake for 15 to 20 minutes, or until lightly browned. Remove from oven and place on wire cooling rack. Let cool.

4. Reduce oven temperature to 375°F.

5. In a large mixing bowl, whisk eggs, sugar, and cornstarch. Add sour cream, lemon juice and rind, and heavy cream. Mix until well blended and smooth. Add pears and stir.

6. Pour batter into cooled crust. Sprinkle top with remaining ¼ cup of pine nuts.

7. Bake for 1 hour and 35 to 40 minutes, or until center is set. Remove pie from the oven and place on wire cooling rack. Cool completely in pan. Remove from pan. Discard parchment. Wrap pie in foil or plastic wrap and refrigerate overnight. Dust with confectioners' sugar and serve chilled.

YIELD: ONE 9-INCH TART, ABOUT 20 SERVINGS

ANTIQUE PIE

PIZZA ANTICO

This crusty "pie" is studded with raisins and nuts. It looks like a large wheel of pastry, impressive and unique, tied with a festive bow. It's the perfect holiday gift—it'll stay fresh for weeks in a cookie tin and actually tastes better with age. Because there are so many inner layers of dough in this pie, it needs to bake for a long time.

CRUST:

2½ TO 3 CUPS FLOUR	6 TABLESPOONS BUTTER, SOFTENED
½ CUP SUGAR	1 EGG
2 TEASPOONS CINNAMON	½ CUP WATER

FILLING:

3 CUPS FINELY CHOPPED WALNUTS	GRATED RIND OF 1 ORANGE
2 CUPS RAISINS	4 TABLESPOONS RUM
2 TEASPOONS CINNAMON	¼ POUND BUTTER
½ TEASPOON NUTMEG	½ CUP HONEY

1. In a food processor, pulse flour, sugar, and cinnamon until uniform. Add butter and process until mixture resembles coarse crumbs. Add egg and water and process.

2. Turn out dough onto a lightly floured surface. Knead until smooth and firm. Wrap dough in plastic wrap and refrigerate overnight.

3. Combine walnuts, raisins, cinnamon, nutmeg, orange rind, and rum in a medium mixing bowl. Stir until well mixed with a wooden spoon.

4. In a small saucepan, stir butter and honey until mixture boils. Remove from the heat. Pour hot honey mixture over nut mixture. Stir to coat evenly. Set aside. Cool completely.

5. Preheat oven to 350°F.

6. Remove dough from the refrigerator. Separate dough into thirds. On a lightly floured surface, roll each third as thin as possible into strips measuring 5 inches wide by 20 to 25 inches long. Trim the edge of each strip with a fluted pastry wheel.

7. Place one third of the filling onto each strip. Fold over each strip to create strips 2½ inches wide by 20 inches long.

8. Starting with one end, roll the filled strips jelly roll fashion into a big "wheel." Add the other two strips to produce one big wheel.

9. Place base of wheel on a parchment-lined cookie sheet.

10. Use cook's twine to tie around middle of torte to be sure it keeps its shape during baking. Tie gently. Brush entire surface with a beaten egg and sprinkle with additional sugar.

11. Bake for 2 hours. Remove pan from the oven. Place torte on wire cooling rack and cool completely. When cool, remove and discard twine. If desired, use a fancy ribbon to replace twine for presentation. Serve when completely cool. Use a sharp serrated knife to cut into slices.

YIELD: ONE 7½-INCH ROUND TORTE, 25 TO 30 SLICES

GRANDMOTHER'S PIE

TORTA DELLA NONNA

I learned to make this classic dessert at "La Tavola con lo Chef" (at the table with the chef), a beautiful cooking school in Rome. It was amazing to observe master baker Nazzareno share his experience and love of pastry with a class of aspiring pastry chefs. Watching his techniques and learning about authentic Italian ingredients was a highlight of my last visit to Rome. His version of pasta frolla uses soft butter in place of chilled and confectioners' sugar instead of granulated.

ITALIAN PASTA FROLLA:

6 TABLESPOONS BUTTER, SOFTENED	PINCH OF SALT
½ CUP CONFECTIONERS' SUGAR	ABOUT ¾ CUP FLOUR
1 EGG YOLK	

ITALIAN PASTRY CREAM:

2 CUPS MILK	⅓ CUP FLOUR
1 CUP SUGAR	1 TEASPOON VANILLA
3 EGG YOLKS	½ CUP PINE NUTS

1. With an electric mixer, cream butter and confectioners' sugar until well blended. Add egg yolk. Mix well. Add salt and flour. Turn out dough onto a lightly floured surface and knead until well blended. Dough should be soft but not sticky. Wrap in plastic wrap. Refrigerate 2 to 3 hours or overnight. You can also freeze for later use.

2. In a medium saucepan over medium heat, bring the milk and ½ cup of sugar to a boil. Remove from the heat. In a separate bowl, beat egg yolks and remaining ½ cup sugar with a wire whisk. Add flour and whisk until smooth.

3. Add egg yolk mixture to milk mixture. Return to medium heat, whisking constantly until thickened, about 2 minutes. Remove from heat. Stir in vanilla. Pour into a bowl, cover top with plastic wrap, and refrigerate, up to one day.

4. Preheat oven to 350°F.

5. Roll out dough on a lightly floured surface until ⅛ inch thick. Line a 9-inch tart pan with removable bottom with the dough.

6. Pour cooled pastry cream into the crust. Sprinkle top with pine nuts.

7. Bake for 30 to 35 minutes, or until lightly browned.

8. Remove from the oven and place on a wire cooling rack. Cool completely. Serve at room temperature. Store unused tart in the refrigerator.

YIELD: ONE 9-INCH TART, ABOUT 8 SERVINGS

SWEET RICOTTA PIE

PIZZA DOLCE

Mom's sweet ricotta pie has always been my favorite way to celebrate Easter.
The smell of this pie cooking is one of my favorite sensory memories.
I had the pleasure of learning to make homemade ricotta cheese with Gemma,
our neighbor who made cheese for a living in Italy. Ricotta was actually the by-product
after we made a batch of delicious soft basket cheese. It didn't yield that much, just a
few tasty tablespoons. We would need to make a huge batch of basket cheese to yield a
significant amount of ricotta, but it was fascinating to see how it's produced.

CRUST:

2 EGGS	1½ TO 1¾ CUPS FLOUR
⅓ CUP SUGAR	PINCH OF SALT
½ CUP MELTED SHORTENING, COOLED	1 TEASPOON BAKING POWDER

FILLING:

6 EGGS	GRATED RIND FROM 1 LEMON
½ CUP SUGAR	3 CUPS RICOTTA
JUICE OF 1 LEMON	

1. For the crust, beat eggs and sugar in an electric mixer until light. Add shortening and mix well. On low speed, gradually add 1¼ cups flour, salt, and baking powder. Turn out dough onto a lightly floured surface. Knead in remaining ¼ to ½ cup flour to make a soft nonsticky dough.

2. Divide dough in half. Using a rolling pin, roll crust on a lightly floured surface to ⅛-inch thickness. Place in an ungreased 9-inch deep-dish pie plate.

3. Roll out remaining dough to the same thickness. Using a fluted-edge pastry cutter, cut dough into strips about ½ inch wide. Set aside and cover with plastic.

4. Preheat oven to 350°F.

5. For the filling, beat eggs in an electric mixer on medium speed. Add sugar, lemon juice, and rind. Beat until well blended. Add ricotta. Blend until smooth.

6. Pour filling into pan lined with bottom crust. Carefully arrange strips of dough to form lattice across the top.

7. Bake for 55 to 60 minutes, or until center is just set. Turn oven off. Leave pie in the oven for 15 minutes.

8. Remove pie from the oven. Cool on wire cooling rack. Refrigerate until serving. Serve chilled.

YIELD: ONE 9-INCH PIE, ABOUT 20 SERVINGS

◆ AL DENTE ◆

THIS TERM REFERS TO COOKING PASTA AND RICE. MOST ITALIANS PRE-FER THEIR PASTA AND RICE FIRMER AND SLIGHTLY MORE UNDERCOOKED THAN DO MOST AMERICANS. FOR OUR RICE PIE YOU'LL WANT TO COOK THE RICE A LITTLE FIRM, A BIT HARDER THAN YOU WOULD IF YOU WERE EATING IT RIGHT AWAY. THE RICE WILL CONTINUE TO COOK IN THE PIE.

EASTER RICE PIE

This crustless Easter pie was my grandmother's specialty. She never really liked pie crusts so she adapted her family recipe to suit her own tastes. The result is a delicious baked rice custard topped with a sprinkle of cinnamon. Be sure to leave the rice a bit undercooked when you make it. It will continue to cook in the pie. You can easily double this recipe and make an 11 x 9-inch pan rice pie if you have a large gathering for Easter. We always do.

2 CUPS WATER	2 TEASPOONS VANILLA
½ CUP RICE	2 CUPS RICOTTA
4 EGGS	1 CUP MILK
¾ CUP SUGAR	2 TEASPOONS CINNAMON

1. In a medium saucepan, bring water to a boil over medium heat. Add rice. Reduce heat to low and cook until al dente, about 20 minutes.

2. Remove from the heat. Drain rice and cool.

3. Preheat oven to 400°F.

4. In an electric mixer on medium speed, beat eggs. Add sugar and vanilla. Add ricotta and beat until smooth.

5. Stir in milk and cooled rice. Pour into ungreased 9-inch round cake pan. Sprinkle cinnamon on top of rice mixture. Carefully place in oven. Bake for 50 to 55 minutes, or until center is just about set.

6. Remove pie from the oven. Cool on wire cooling rack. Refrigerate until serving. Serve chilled.

YIELD: ONE 9-INCH PIE, ABOUT 12 SERVINGS

AUNT ERNESTINE'S CREAM PIE

This unique pie is a specialty of my grandmother's family, the Palmieris. It has an unusual combination of pastry cream, cherry filling, and apricots that sounds odd but tastes delicious when chilled and served. You can make several of the components ahead of time. Just store the pasta frolla, pastry cream, and sour cherry filling in the refrigerator before assembling the pie.

1 RECIPE PASTA FROLLA (SEE PAGE 78)

1 RECIPE SOUR CHERRY FILLING (SEE FOLLOWING RECIPE)

1 RECIPE VANILLA PASTRY CREAM (SEE FOLLOWING RECIPE)

16 OUNCES APRICOT HALVES, PEELED

1. Make pasta frolla according to directions. Divide dough in half. Wrap each half in plastic wrap and refrigerate for 3 hours or overnight.

2. Preheat oven to 375°F.

3. Roll out half the pasta frolla on a lightly floured surface until ⅛ inch thick. Line a greased 9-inch deep-dish pie plate with crust. Press into plate. Let excess hang over.

4. Spread cherry filling on the bottom of the crust. Spread vanilla cream filling over cherries. Place peeled apricots evenly on pastry cream.

5. Roll out remaining half of pasta frolla until ⅛ inch thick. Cover apricots to form a top crust. Use fingers to pinch edges together to seal crusts together. Be sure to tuck edges in so that they do not hang over the rim.

6. Bake for 55 to 60 minutes, until center is golden brown. Remove pie from the oven. Cool on wire cooling rack. When cool, cover with plastic wrap or foil and refrigerate overnight. Serve chilled.

YIELD: ONE 9-INCH PIE, ABOUT 15 SERVINGS

SOUR CHERRY FILLING

1 POUND (16 OUNCES) SOUR PITTED
CHERRIES, PACKED IN WATER, DRAINED

¾ CUP SUGAR

In a small saucepan over low heat, combine cherries and sugar. Simmer, stirring occasionally, until thick and maroon colored, about 50 minutes. Remove from heat. Cool. Set aside.

VANILLA PASTRY CREAM

¼ CUP FLOUR

1 TABLESPOON CORNSTARCH

1 CUP SUGAR

3 CUPS MILK

6 EGG YOLKS, SLIGHTLY BEATEN

1 TEASPOON VANILLA

1. In a mixing bowl over water or double boiler over medium heat, blend together all pastry cream ingredients, except vanilla. Whisk constantly over boiling water until thick, 20 to 25 minutes.

2. Remove from the heat. Stir in vanilla. Set aside to cool.

PASTRY

◆ ◆ ◆

Italian pastry is well known as being some of the world's best. Many of these techniques have been handed down through generations of bakers. In this section I've chosen to include some of the easiest recipes to make at home. They include fried pastries, baked puffs, and miniature pies and cakes that are served as individual desserts.

There are many ways to serve these desserts. Here are a few suggestions:

Place a few tablespoons of fruit or chocolate sauce on the serving dish.

Place a slice of cake or pastry in the center and sprinkle outer edge of plate with a dusting of confectioners' sugar or edible flowers.

Drizzle chocolate sauce or fruit sauce with a fork with light swinging motion over pastry.

Serve with a simple dollop of whipped cream, a chocolate chunk, or assorted fresh fruits arranged on top or to the side.

Use sweet herbs like mint or lavender to garnish.

Use candied citrus peels.

MOCHA CREAM PUFFS
BIGNE

These puffs are international favorites that I've filled with a tasty coffee and chocolate cream filling. Try them simply dusted with confectioners' sugar or drizzled with a chocolate fudge sauce. For freshness, try to fill them as close to serving time as possible. Use this recipe to create small or large cream puffs or éclairs. Be sure to have your eggs at room temperature before adding to the hot dough.

CREAM PUFFS:

7 TABLESPOONS BUTTER	1 CUP FLOUR
1 CUP WATER	4 EGGS, AT ROOM TEMPERATURE
PINCH OF SALT	

MOCHA CREAM:

2 CUPS HEAVY CREAM	1 TEASPOON INSTANT ESPRESSO COFFEE
5 TABLESPOONS COCOA	½ CUP SUGAR

1. Preheat oven to 450°F.

2. In a medium saucepan over medium-high heat, combine butter, water, and salt. Bring to a boil. Add flour quickly, all at once, and stir with a wooden spoon until mixture comes away from the sides of the pan.

3. Remove pan from the heat. In an electric mixer, add eggs, one at a time, mixing well after adding each one. Mix well for a smooth sticky dough. Spoon a heaping tablespoon of hot dough onto a parchment-lined cookie sheet, spacing each about 1 inch apart.

4. Bake for 15 minutes. Reduce heat to 350°F. Continue baking for 30 to 35 minutes, or until golden brown. Remove puffs from the oven. Cool on wire cooling racks.

5. Combine heavy cream, cocoa, espresso, and sugar. With an electric mixer with wire whisk attachment, whip on high speed until soft peaks form, about 2 min-

utes. Scrape down the sides and bottom of mixing bowl using a rubber spatula. Continue whipping on high speed until stiff. Use immediately.

6. Slice the tops of cream puffs off with a serrated knife. Set aside. Using a pastry bag or tablespoon, fill the puffs with cream. Place tops on puffs. Dust with confectioners' sugar and serve. Store in refrigerator. Serve chilled.

YIELD: ABOUT 16 LARGE PUFFS

TRADITIONAL CANNOLI

*These crispy shells, filled with sweetened ricotta, originated in Sicily but are found al-
most everywhere. The secret to making cannoli is to roll the dough very thin and fry the
shells in very hot oil. Fill the shells just before serving. If you do it too far in advance,
the shell will get soggy. You can find many variations of cannoli, some with a chocolate
ricotta, ice cream, or pastry cream filling.*

SHELLS:

1¾ CUPS FLOUR	¾ CUP MARSALA
1 TABLESPOON SUGAR	OIL FOR FRYING
PINCH OF SALT	1 CUP MINI CHOCOLATE CHIPS
2 TABLESPOONS BUTTER, MELTED	GRATED RIND OF 1 LEMON

RICOTTA FILLING:

5 CUPS RICOTTA	GRATED RIND OF 1 ORANGE
1½ CUPS CONFECTIONERS' SUGAR	

1. In a medium mixing bowl, combine flour, sugar, and salt. Add melted butter and marsala. Turn out dough onto a lightly floured surface. Knead until well mixed.

2. Wrap dough in plastic wrap and refrigerate for 2 to 3 hours.

3. Roll out dough until very thin. Using a cookie cutter or rim of a glass, cut dough into 4-inch rounds. After cutting, roll each piece again until very thin. Roll each round tightly around cannoli tube. Seal with egg white.

4. Fry in hot oil, turning with a slotted spoon. Fry until golden brown. Remove from oil and drain on absorbent paper. Cool and gently twist tube to remove shell from form.

5. Cool completely before filling.

6. In a medium mixing bowl, stir all filling ingredients with a wooden spoon to mix together. Refrigerate until using. Store unused filling in an airtight container in refrigerator.

7. Fill a pastry bag fitted with a plain or open star tip with ricotta filling. Grab the shell and press tip of pastry bag toward middle of the shell. Press bag to release filling into one side of the shell. Repeat with other side.

8. Continue to fill the shells as needed. Dust with confectioners' sugar and serve. Store filled cannolis wrapped in plastic wrap or foil in refrigerator. Store unfilled shells in an airtight container at room temperature for 2 to 3 days.

YIELD: ABOUT 16 CANNOLI

RUM SPONGE CAKES

*These light little sponge cakes are generously soaked in a sweet rum syrup,
similar to the traditional "rum baba." They make a precious dessert for a
small dinner party. You can serve one per person or one per couple. You'll need
to have four mini tube pans to bake these cakes. They measure about 4 inches
in diameter and are usually sold in a set of four.*

MINI SPONGE CAKES:

4 EGG WHITES	4 EGG YOLKS
½ CUP PLUS 2 TABLESPOONS SUGAR	½ TEASPOON VANILLA EXTRACT
¼ TEASPOON CREAM OF TARTAR	¾ CUP CAKE FLOUR
¼ TEASPOON SALT	2 TABLESPOONS COLD WATER

RUM SYRUP:

1 CUP WATER	1 CUP SUGAR
½ CUP LIGHT OR DARK RUM	2 CUPS ASSORTED BERRIES

1. Preheat oven to 325°F.

2. In an electric mixer with wire whisk attachment, beat egg whites, 2 tablespoons of sugar, cream of tartar, and salt. Start on medium speed, then use high speed until very stiff peaks form, 3 to 4 minutes. Set aside.

3. In a separate bowl, with an electric mixer on medium speed, beat the egg yolks, ½ cup sugar, and vanilla. Beat until light in color, 2 to 3 minutes.

4. Alternate adding flour and water to egg yolk mixture. Begin and end with flour. Mix just until blended.

5. Using a rubber spatula, fold egg yolk mixture into beaten whites. When blended, spoon batter evenly into four 4-inch ungreased mini tube pans.

6. Bake for 20 to 25 minutes, or until lightly browned. Remove pan from the oven.

7. Cool cakes in pan on wire cooling rack.

8. When completely cool, carefully remove cakes from the pan. Use a sharp straight knife to loosen the outside and inner tube of the cake from the pan.

9. Prepare rum syrup or store cakes in plastic wrap overnight at room temperature. Cakes can also be frozen for later use.

10. In a small saucepan, bring water to a boil. Add sugar. Boil on medium-high heat until sugar is dissolved and mixture becomes syrupy, 12 to 15 minutes. Remove from the heat. Stir in rum. Use immediately.

11. Pour a quarter of the rum syrup into a medium baking dish. Place sponge cakes, bottom side down, in syrup.

12. Evenly pour the remaining rum syrup over the cakes. Cover cakes with plastic wrap and refrigerate. Let soak for 2 to 3 hours or overnight.

13. Spoon ½ cup fresh fruit over each cake and serve.

YIELD: 4 MINI SPONGE CAKES, ABOUT 4 SERVINGS

LITTLE MOUTHFULS
BOCCONCINI

These little pies are filled with a sweetened ricotta, cinnamon, and chopped walnuts. This is my comare (godmother) Gloria's recipe, a specialty of her family from the town of Bari. If you don't have a 4½-inch cookie cutter, use the rim of a glass. Even though it's not Italian, I use a margarita glass—it's the perfect size.

CRUST:

2 CUPS FLOUR	¼ POUND BUTTER
½ CUP SUGAR	3 EGG YOLKS
GRATED RIND OF 1 LEMON	½ CUP MILK
½ TEASPOON BAKING POWDER	

FILLING:

3 CUPS RICOTTA	½ CUP SUGAR
2 EGGS	

TOPPING:

4 TABLESPOONS SUGAR	4 TABLESPOONS FINELY CHOPPED WALNUTS
1 TEASPOON CINNAMON	

1. Combine flour, sugar, lemon rind, and baking powder in a food processor. Pulse until blended. Add butter and process until mixture resembles coarse crumbs. Add egg yolks and milk and process to form a dough.

2. Turn out dough onto a lightly floured surface. Knead until well mixed. Dough should be soft but not sticky. Wrap in plastic wrap and refrigerate for 2 hours or overnight.

3. In a medium mixing bowl, combine ricotta, eggs, and sugar. Stir with a rubber spatula until well blended. Refrigerate until using.

4. Preheat oven to 375°F.

5. Grease and flour a standard muffin pan or spray with a nonstick spray. Set aside.

6. On a lightly floured surface, roll out dough until ⅛ inch thick. Cut dough into 4½-inch circles. Press dough circle into prepared muffin pan. Line the pan and form a lip or small pie crust around the edge of each. Repeat until all dough is used.

7. Spoon filling into crusts, until just about full.

8. In a small bowl, combine sugar, cinnamon, and walnuts. Sprinkle filling with cinnamon sugar and walnut mixture.

9. Bake for 25 to 30 minutes, or until middle is set. These will puff up in the center during baking but will fall when cooled.

10. Remove pan from the oven. Cool bocconcini in pan on wire rack. When cool, use a fork to remove from pans. Refrigerate until serving. Serve chilled.

YIELD: 12 BOCCONCINI

◆ TRAVELING PASTRY CHEFS ◆

MANY ITALIAN PASTRY CHEFS TRAVELED WITH CATHERINE DE MÉDICI WHEN SHE WENT TO LIVE IN FRANCE. IT WAS THESE CHEFS WHO SHOWED THE FRENCH CHEFS SOME OF THEIR BASIC TECHNIQUES FOR PASTRY MAKING, WHICH THEY THEN ADAPTED TO MAKE SOME OF THEIR LEGENDARY SWEETS.

BUTTERFLIES

FARFALLE

These little sweet, fried pastries stay crispy for days. They are rolled and then cut to form a bow or butterfly shape. The thinner you roll the dough, the crisper and lighter the butterflies will be.

3 EGG YOLKS

½ CUP SUGAR

½ CUP MILK

2 TEASPOONS VANILLA EXTRACT

2 CUPS FLOUR

OIL FOR FRYING

1. In a medium mixing bowl, whisk egg yolks with a wire whisk. Add sugar and mix until light. Add milk and vanilla. With a wooden spoon, mix in 1½ cups flour.

2. Turn out dough onto a floured surface. Knead in remaining ½ cup flour to make a stiff nonsticky dough.

3. Divide dough in half. Roll one half out with a rolling pin on a lightly floured surface. Roll as thin as possible. Using a fluted pastry cutter, cut dough into strips that measure about 3 x 2 inches. Pinch the dough in the center to form a bow tie. Roll all of the dough, saving all the scraps to reroll at the end.

4. In a medium saucepan, heat about 1 inch of vegetable oil. Fry the butterflies, without crowding the pan, until golden brown. Turn using a slotted spoon or tongs. Remove from the oil and drain on absorbent paper.

5. Cool and dust with confectioners' sugar. Store unused butterflies in an airtight container at room temperature.

YIELD: ABOUT 25 BUTTERFLIES

LEMON RICOTTA FRITTERS

SFINGI DI RICOTTA

These fresh little puffs are like a delicious doughnut. They taste best when freshly fried and slightly warm. Serve with a dusting of confectioners' sugar and a drizzle of fruit sauce for a simple, elegant dessert.

2 EGGS, BEATEN

2 TABLESPOONS SUGAR

1 CUP RICOTTA

2 TABLESPOONS LEMON JUICE

LEMON RIND

¾ CUP FLOUR

1 TEASPOON BAKING POWDER

PINCH OF SALT

OIL FOR FRYING

1. In an electric mixer, beat eggs. Add sugar and ricotta. Mix until well blended. Add lemon juice and rind. Blend in flour, baking powder, and salt. Transfer mixture to a medium bowl. Cover and refrigerate for 1 hour.

2. Heat about 1 inch of vegetable oil over medium heat in a medium saucepan. Using a teaspoon, drop dough into hot oil. Fry until golden brown, turning with a fork. Use a slotted spoon to remove fritters from the hot oil. Drain on absorbent paper. Dust with confectioners' sugar. Serve immediately.

YIELD: 20 FRITTERS

PASTICIOTTE

These popular little pies are filled with vanilla pastry cream. You can find many variations in Italian pastry shops. Some have chocolate filling or ricotta filling. My dad and I agree that this vanilla-filled version is our favorite. Dad loves them with a cup of espresso with a splash of Sambuca.

To make the crust, use either a pastry blender or food processor.

CRUST:

2½ CUPS FLOUR	¼ CUP WATER
¾ CUP SUGAR	1 EGG
½ TEASPOON BAKING POWDER	2 TABLESPOONS HONEY
¾ CUP SHORTENING	

FILLING:

2½ CUPS MILK	¼ CUP FLOUR
¾ CUP SUGAR	2 TABLESPOONS CORNSTARCH
2 EGG YOLKS	1 TEASPOON VANILLA

1. Preheat oven to 350°F.

2. In a medium mixing bowl, combine flour, sugar, and baking powder. Using a pastry blender, blend in shortening until the mixture resembles coarse crumbs. Add water, egg, and honey. Stir with a wooden spoon. Turn out dough onto a lightly floured surface and knead until well blended. Divide dough in half and wrap dough in plastic wrap and set aside.

3. Make filling. In a double boiler or pan over simmering water, combine milk, sugar, egg yolks, flour, and cornstarch. Whisk over heat until thickened, about 10 to 12 minutes. Remove from the heat. Stir in vanilla. Set aside.

4. Using a rolling pin, roll out one half of the dough on a lightly floured surface. Roll until about ⅛ inch thick. Cut dough into 4-inch rounds using a cookie cutter or rim of a glass.

5. Press a round of dough into a greased muffin pan.

6. Using a tablespoon, fill each dough with about 2 tablespoons of filling. Roll out another set of 4-inch dough rounds. Use these circles to top the filling. Pinch outer edge of the crusts together. Repeat until all circles are filled.

7. Bake for 25 minutes, or until golden brown. Remove from the oven. Cool slightly in pan on wire cooling rack. When cool to touch, carefully remove each pasticiotte from the pan and continue to cool on wire rack. Serve at room temperature or refrigerate and serve chilled. Dust with confectioners' sugar.

YIELD: 12 PASTICIOTTE

◆ BAKERIES IN ITALY ◆

THERE ARE MANY TYPES OF SHOPS IN ITALY THAT CAN BE CLASSIFIED AS WHAT WE CALL BAKERIES. SOME SHOPS SELL BREAD, ROLLS, SWEET BAKED GOODS, AND DELI ITEMS. THESE ARE USUALLY TAKE-OUT SHOPS. OTHERS ARE HIGH-QUALITY PASTRY SHOPS KNOWN AS *PASTICCERIA*. THESE SHOPS HAVE A DIVERSE SELECTION OF PASTRIES AND CAKES, AND SOMETIMES GELATO. YOU CAN USUALLY EAT IN OR TAKE OUT. WHEN YOU TAKE OUT, YOU PICK WHAT YOU'D LIKE AND THEY WRAP IT BEAUTIFULLY. YOU MUST PAY A CASHIER AND THEN GO BACK AND PICK UP YOUR PACKAGE.

THERE ARE ALSO BARS THAT SERVE PASTRY, COFFEE, AND ALCOHOLIC BEVERAGES. AND *TAVOLA CALDA*, WHICH MEANS "HOT TABLE." THESE ARE QUICK-BITE PLACES THAT SERVE SANDWICHES, PIZZA, FOCCACCIA, SWEET BAKED ITEMS, COFFEE, AND ALCOHOLIC BEVERAGES. YOU CAN EITHER SIT AT A TABLE FOR AN ADDITIONAL CHARGE, OR STAND UP AND EAT. OBVIOUSLY, SWEETS ARE VERY IMPORTANT—YOU CAN FIND THEM JUST ABOUT EVERYWHERE IN ITALY.

FIG AND MASCARPONE RAVIOLI

*These triangle-shaped ravioli are fried and dusted with confectioners' sugar. To elimi-
nate the need to make a crust, you can use wonton wrappers (you can use wonton wrappers for traditional ravioli as well). These treats are easy to make—in fact, you can fill
them about 8 hours before you fry them.*

8 OUNCES MASCARPONE CHEESE

¼ CUP CONFECTIONERS' SUGAR

1 TEASPOON AMARETTO

1 CUP DRIED FIGS, COARSELY
CHOPPED

20 3-INCH-SQUARE WONTON WRAP-
PERS

1 EGG FOR SEALING

OIL FOR FRYING

1. In an electric mixer, cream the mascarpone and confectioners' sugar until well
   blended. Stir in amaretto and chopped figs. Set aside.

2. Place all the wonton wrappers on a work surface. Brush the edges of each square
   with beaten egg. Place 1 generous tablespoon of filling in the center of each
   square. Fold wrapper over to form triangle. Press edges together until sealed. Repeat filling and sealing all the wrappers. Cover and refrigerate 2 to 4 hours.

3. Fry ravioli, a few at a time, in hot oil. Turn with a slotted spoon. Fry until golden
   brown. Remove from the oil with a slotted spoon and drain on absorbent paper.
   Dust with confectioners' sugar or serve with dessert sauce. Serve warm or cooled.

YIELD: 20 RAVIOLI

SWEET BREADS

♦ ♦ ♦

Many people, myself included, are intimidated by the thought of baking bread that includes yeast. However, with today's easily available active dry yeast, breads can be almost foolproof. I hope you'll try some of these sweet breads—there's nothing quite like the sweet yeasty smell of Easter bread baking, and its perfect taste served warm from the oven with a chunk of butter. It reminds me so much of my childhood and the pending season of spring that always comes after the Easter celebration.

Here are a few tips and general guidelines for baking the sweet breads in this section.

Activating Dry Yeast

It is important that you use lukewarm water, as directed in the recipes, to activate yeast. Water that is too hot will kill the yeast. Water that is too cold will not activate it.

Rising in a Warm Place

Every home bread baker I know has their own personal place for rising bread. My friend Betsy uses a really sunny window in her upstairs bedroom. For me, it's the top of my gas stove at home. If the oven is heated to 375°F the right amount of heat will be vented out onto the top of the stove. I usually place my bread dough here, in a mixing bowl covered with plastic wrap and a dish towel, right between the burners to catch the escaping hot air. A warmed oven, not too hot, 70 to 80°F, is ideal as well.

Doubled in Bulk

This is a widely used term to describe how much the dough has risen. Usually, every time you let the dough rise you're looking for it to be double the size of when you began. Many of the rising times in these recipes are approximate, depending on how warm your warming spot is. You can't be in a hurry to bake bread. You must be sure you've allowed proper time for rising.

Kneading or Punching Down the Dough

Kneading and punching down the dough are important steps to mix and work the dough to its proper consistency.

Storage

Home-baked breads can become stale easily. Be sure to wrap cooled, unused bread in a plastic bag. Store at room temperature for a few days or freeze for later use. Bread that is a couple of days old makes great toast for your breakfast or bread pudding. Do not store bread in the refrigerator. This will make it get stale quicker.

ANISE BREAD

PANE D'ANISE

This dense ring-shaped loaf is a nice breakfast or snack bread. For the strongest anise flavor, use an anise oil or extract. If you like a softer flavor, substitute 2 tablespoons anisette or Sambuca in place of the extract.

1 PACKAGE ACTIVE DRY YEAST

½ CUP LUKEWARM WATER

¼ POUND BUTTER, SOFTENED

1 CUP SUGAR

2 EGGS, PLUS 1 ADDITIONAL EGG FOR EGG WASH

2 TEASPOONS ANISE EXTRACT (OR 2 TABLESPOONS ANISETTE)

3 CUPS FLOUR

PINCH OF SALT

1. In a small bowl, mix yeast with lukewarm water. Set aside.

2. In an electric mixer on medium speed, cream butter and ½ cup sugar until light. Add eggs and anise extract. Mix well. Add 1½ cups flour, salt, and yeast mixture. Mix just until blended. Cover bowl with plastic wrap and a towel and let rise until doubled in bulk, 45 minutes to 1 hour.

3. Stir in remaining ½ cup sugar and 1½ cups flour. Turn out dough onto a lightly floured surface and knead until dough is soft and smooth. If dough is sticky, knead in a bit more flour. Form dough into a ball. Place in a greased mixing bowl. Cover with plastic wrap and a towel. Let rise until doubled in bulk, 45 minutes to 1 hour.

4. Roll and shape dough into a cylinder about 30 inches long. Form into a ring shape and place on a parchment-lined cookie sheet. Be sure to pinch ends together to form a uniformly wide ring. Cover with plastic wrap and a towel and allow to rise in a warm spot for another 35 to 40 minutes.

5. Preheat oven to 325°F.

6. In a small bowl, beat egg with a fork. With a pastry brush, brush top of loaf with beaten egg. Bake for 25 to 30 minutes, or until top is lightly brown. Remove from the oven. Cool on wire cooling rack. Serve warm or cooled. Store unused bread in plastic bag at room temperature for a few days or freeze for later use.

YIELD: ONE 10-INCH RING-SHAPED LOAF, ABOUT 25 SLICES

EASTER BREAD

PANE DI PASQUA

This is my godmother Gloria's new and improved Easter bread. She originally had to let this dough rise overnight, which to me seems like a long time. By changing her original recipe to a sponge method, I've cut down the length of time the bread will take to rise. It's still the same delicious bread, served either plain or toasted.

2 PACKAGES ACTIVE DRY YEAST	GRATED RIND OF 1 LEMON
¼ CUP LUKEWARM WATER	½ CUP SHORTENING, MELTED
6 EGGS	4 TO 4½ CUPS FLOUR
1 CUP SUGAR	

1. Dissolve yeast in lukewarm water. Set aside.

2. In an electric mixer, beat eggs. Add ½ cup of sugar and lemon rind. Add melted cooled shortening. Mix well. With a wooden spoon, stir in 2 cups flour and yeast mixture. Mix until well blended. Cover top of bowl with plastic wrap and a towel. Let mixture rise in a warm spot, free from drafts until doubled and bubbly, 30 to 45 minutes.

3. Remove dough from warming spot. Stir in the remaining ½ cup sugar and 2 cups of flour. Turn out dough onto a lightly floured surface and knead in enough flour for a soft dough, about ½ cup. The dough should not be too sticky.

4. Grease a large mixing bowl. Place dough in the greased bowl. Cover top with plastic wrap and a towel and return to warm spot until doubled in bulk, 45 to 60 minutes.

5. Grease a 10-inch tube pan with removable bottom with butter. Turn out dough on a lightly floured surface. Knead. Roll dough into a long cylinder and place in prepared pan. Cover pan with plastic wrap and a towel and allow to rise again in a warm spot. Let rise until doubled, about 30 minutes. Remove and discard plastic wrap.

6. Preheat oven to 300°F.

7. Bake bread for 30 to 35 minutes, or until golden brown and firm.

8. Remove pan from the oven. Cool pan slightly on wire rack. Carefully remove bread from the pan and continue to cool on wire cooling rack.

9. Serve warm or cool. Serve plain or frost top with lemon confectioners' icing. Store cool unused bread in a plastic bag at room temperature.

YIELD: ONE 10-INCH TUBE PAN, 25 TO 30 SLICES

BRAIDED EASTER BREAD
WITH EGGS
PANE DI PASQUA CON UOVO

This recipe makes a beautiful braided ring-shaped loaf. It can be a festive Easter centerpiece; just place in a basket surrounded by shredded paper grass and jelly beans. The eggs become hard-boiled as you bake the bread, making it the perfect Easter breakfast—eggs and bread.

1 PACKAGE ACTIVE DRY YEAST	JUICE AND GRATED RIND OF 1 LEMON
½ CUP LUKEWARM WATER	¼ TEASPOON SALT
2 TO 2½ CUPS FLOUR	1 EGG
¾ STICK BUTTER, SOFTENED	4 WHOLE UNCOOKED EGGS, PLAIN OR
½ CUP SUGAR	COLORED FOR EASTER

1. In a small bowl, dissolve yeast in ¼ cup of lukewarm water. Set aside.

2. In a medium mixing bowl, add remaining water and 1 cup flour. Using an electric mixer, mix in yeast until well blended and smooth. Cover bowl with plastic wrap and a towel and place in a warm place to rise, 1 to 2 hours. This mixture should double in bulk.

3. In an electric mixer, cream butter. Gradually add sugar and beat until light. Add lemon juice and rind and salt. Add egg.

4. Add raised yeast mixture and mix well.

5. With a wooden spoon, stir in about 1 to 1½ cups of flour. Turn dough out onto a floured surface and knead to form a soft non-sticky dough. Shape into a ball. Place dough in a greased bowl. Cover with plastic wrap and a towel and let rise in a warm place until doubled in bulk, about 2 hours.

6. Punch down the dough with your fist. Divide the dough into 2 equal pieces. Roll each piece of dough into a long cylinder about 1½ inches thick.

7. Loosely twist two pieces of dough together to form a loose braid. Form the braid into a ring shape and place on a parchment-lined cookie sheet. Place uncooked eggs into spaces in braid. Cover with plastic wrap and a towel and let rise until doubled in a warm spot, about 40 minutes. Remove plastic wrap and towel.

8. Preheat oven to 375°F.

9. Bake for 25 to 30 minutes, or until golden brown.

10. Remove from the oven. Cool bread in a pan on wire rack. Serve warm or cold. When cool, if desired, frost top of loaf with confectioners' frosting.

YIELD: ONE BRAIDED LOAF, ABOUT 20 SLICES

CHRISTMAS FRUIT BREAD
PANETTONE

This is a traditional Italian sweet bread that is ideal for breakfast, either plain or toasted. This version with chopped dates and lemon and orange rind has a fresh contemporary flavor. When my mom bakes bread she uses an old fur-collared winter coat to help keep the dough warm while it rises.

2 PACKAGES ACTIVE DRY YEAST

1 CUP LUKEWARM WATER

¼ POUND BUTTER, MELTED AND COOLED

4 EGGS

2 TEASPOONS SALT

½ CUP SUGAR

GRATED RIND OF 1 LEMON

GRATED RIND OF 1 ORANGE

5 TO 5½ CUPS FLOUR, APPROXIMATELY

½ CUP CHOPPED DATES

1 CUP GOLDEN RAISINS

1 TABLESPOON BUTTER, MELTED

CONFECTIONERS' ICING, IF DESIRED

1. Grease and line a 10 x 3-inch cake pan with baking parchment. Let the paper measure 3 inches above the side of pan, forming a collar. Set aside.

2. In a small bowl, sprinkle yeast over lukewarm water. Set aside.

3. In an electric mixer, beat butter, eggs, salt, sugar, lemon rind, and orange rind. Using a wooden spoon, add yeast mixture and 4 cups of flour. Turn out dough onto a lightly floured surface. Knead dough until not sticky, adding remaining 1 to 1½ cups flour.

4. Knead in dates and raisins. Place dough in a large greased bowl. Cover with plastic wrap and towels and set in a warm place. Let dough rise until doubled in bulk, 1½ to 2 hours.

5. Remove dough from bowl and knead on a lightly floured surface. Form dough into a ball. Place dough into prepared pan.

6. Using a sharp serrated knife, cut a cross in the top of the dough. Brush the top of the dough with melted butter.

7. Cover with plastic wrap and a towel and set dough to rise in a warm spot until doubled again, 30 to 45 minutes.

8. Preheat oven to 425°F.

9. Remove plastic wrap and bake bread until top browns, about 10 minutes. Reduce oven temperature to 325°F. Bake for 35 to 40 minutes, or until golden brown and firm.

10. Remove from oven and cool on wire rack for 10 to 15 minutes. Carefully remove panettone from the pan and continue to cool on wire rack. Remove and discard parchment. Frost with confectioners' icing or serve plain. Store unused bread in plastic at room temperature or freeze.

YIELD: ONE 10-INCH LOAF, ABOUT 25 SLICES

FROZEN DESSERTS

Frozen desserts and gelato (Italian ice cream) are hugely popular throughout Italy. There are so many flavors to choose from in Italian gelaterias—everything from lemon, pineapple, watermelon, and kiwi to coffee, pistachio, zabaglione, and cassata. Gelati are commonly served in cups or cones or in a small dish accompanied by a biscotti or two. (If you've made the biscotti yourself, so much the better!)

Many of the frozen desserts included in this section can be made ahead, put in the freezer, and taken out little by little to enjoy. They make perfect endings for company, either planned or unexpected.

Many of the molded frozen desserts, such as Zuccotto and Semi-Freddo, require you to grease and line the bowl or mold with plastic wrap. This will allow for easy unmolding of these desserts. To unmold, set frozen dessert in a large pan of hot water for a few minutes. Turn dessert upside down onto a serving plate or doily-covered cake circle to release.

Ice Cream Makers

For some of these recipes you'll need an ice cream maker. I have an inexpensive one that has a frozen insert that is stored in the freezer. To use it I simply add chilled ice cream ingredients and turn the handle twice every 5 minutes for about 20 minutes. It's really simple. This type of maker will work fine. For the fancier electric makers, follow the manufacturer's instructions.

APRICOT ALMOND SEMI-FREDDO

This half or partly frozen loaf-shaped dessert is very flavorful and rich in texture. Be sure to use a high-quality sipping liqueur in this recipe for the fullest flavor. Try it served plain or drizzled with a rich chocolate sauce.

½ CUP DRIED APRICOTS, CHOPPED

4 EGG YOLKS

6 TABLESPOONS SUGAR

¼ CUP AMARETTO

2½ CUPS HEAVY CREAM

½ CUP SLICED ALMONDS, TOASTED

1. Place dried apricots in a small saucepan. Cover with water and boil over high heat until tender, about 15 minutes. Remove from heat. Drain and cool. Purée in food processor. Set aside.

2. Line a large loaf pan (8 x 4 inches) with plastic wrap. Let the wrap hang over the sides about 3 inches. Place in freezer to chill.

3. In a double boiler, over simmering water, whisk egg yolks, sugar, and amaretto until thick and foamy, 5 to 6 minutes. Remove from the heat.

4. In an electric mixer with wire whisk, whip heavy cream until stiff, 2 to 3 minutes.

5. Fold in egg yolk mixture, apricots, and almonds.

6. Pour into prepared pan. Cover bottom of pan with excess plastic wrap. Freeze overnight.

7. Slice into pieces and serve frozen. Store unused semi-freddo wrapped in plastic in freezer.

YIELD: ONE LOAF, ABOUT 12 SLICES

PISTACHIO DOME

ZUCCOTTO

This dome-shaped ice cream cake is impressive and easy to assemble. You can use your mixer bowl for a mold, to give the cake a nice height. Or you can use a mold that is about 7 inches wide by 9 inches tall.

1 RECIPE POUND CAKE (SEE PAGE 44)   GARNISH: COCOA FOR DUSTING

1 QUART PISTACHIO ICE CREAM

1 RECIPE CHOCOLATE WHIPPED CREAM
(SEE FOLLOWING RECIPE)

1. Grease and line mixer bowl or mold with plastic wrap. Let plastic wrap hang 4 to 5 inches out of the bowl. Set aside.

2. Cut pound cake into ½-inch slices. Then cut each slice in half diagonally to form triangles. Line the inside of the mold with triangle slices with points toward the top of the mold. Fit the slices snug so that the mold is completely lined. Use small pieces of cake to fill in gaps where necessary.

3. Scoop pistachio ice cream into the mold, pressing it against the walls of the mold but leaving a well in the center.

4. Spoon chocolate whipped cream into the center of the mold. Press down firmly with the back of a spoon to avoid any air pockets. Cover with any remaining slices of cake. (Be sure this is level before freezing. When you invert the mold, it will become the bottom of the zuccotto.) Cover with excess plastic wrap.

5. Freeze overnight. To unmold, place mold in a bowl of hot water for a few minutes. Invert onto a serving plate or doily-covered cake circle. Dust with cocoa before serving. Let zuccotto stay at room temperature to soften slightly, 15 to 20 minutes, before slicing with a sharp straight knife. Serve frozen. Store unused zuccotto wrapped in plastic in the freezer.

YIELD: ONE ZUCCOTTO, ABOUT 20 SERVINGS

CHOCOLATE WHIPPED CREAM

2 CUPS HEAVY CREAM

½ CUP COCOA

½ CUP SUGAR

In an electric mixer with wire whisk attachment, beat all ingredients until stiff. Set aside.

VANILLA TORTONI

These ice cream cupcakes are great fun for children to make and eat. Make a batch together and take out a few at a time for dessert. Before freezing, decorate tops with colorful sprinkles or nonpareils.

1 CUP HEAVY CREAM	½ CUP WALNUTS, CHOPPED
3 EGGS	½ CUP MARASCHINO CHERRIES, CHOPPED
⅔ CUP SUGAR	
2 TEASPOONS VANILLA	¼ CUP GRAHAM CRACKER CRUMBS

1. In an electric mixer with a wire whisk attachment, beat heavy cream until stiff. Set aside.

2. In another bowl, beat eggs and sugar until light. Add vanilla. Fold in whipped heavy cream, nuts, and cherries.

3. Place 12 paper dessert cups on a cookie sheet. Pour cream mixture evenly into paper cups. Sprinkle the tops with graham cracker crumbs. Place cookie sheet in the freezer. Freeze overnight. Serve frozen. Wrap unused tortoni in foil or plastic wrap and store in the freezer for up to 1 month.

YIELD: 12 CUPCAKE-SIZE TORTONI

COFFEE ICE WITH CREAM
GRANITA DI CAFFE

A popular summer treat in Italy, granita is a frozen shaved ice that comes in many flavors. This coffee and cream version is my favorite.

1 CUP WATER

½ CUP SUGAR

1 CUP DOUBLE-STRENGTH BREWED
ESPRESSO

½ CUP HEAVY CREAM

1. In a small saucepan over medium-high heat, combine water and sugar. Stir until boiling. Let boil for about 1 minute, or until sugar dissolves. Remove from the heat. Stir in espresso.

2. Pour mixture into a medium stainless steel bowl. Place bowl in the freezer for about 3 hours.

3. Remove coffee mixture from the freezer. Use a fork to shave flakes of ice off the coffee mixture. Spoon flaked mixture into individual serving cups or place flakes in another bowl. Freeze until ready to serve.

4. Just before serving, whip cream until stiff. Spoon cream over the top of shaved granita and serve.

YIELD: EIGHT ½-CUP SERVINGS

GRAPEFRUIT SORBET
SORBETO DI POMPELMO

This flexible recipe can be made in other flavors. Simply substitute any type of fruit juice for the grapefruit juice. This sorbet is perfect when it is soft and freshly made, or firmer after it is stored in the freezer.

3 CUPS GRAPEFRUIT JUICE   2 TABLESPOONS CORN SYRUP

1 CUP SUGAR

1. In a medium saucepan, combine 1 cup grapefruit juice, sugar, and corn syrup over medium heat. Heat, stirring occasionally, until sugar dissolves. Remove from the heat.

2. Stir in remaining 2 cups of grapefruit juice. Pour into a bowl and refrigerate for 3 to 4 hours or overnight.

3. Pour juice mixture into an ice cream maker. Process according to instructions. When frozen, serve soft or store in the freezer in an airtight container until firmer. Serve frozen.

YIELD: EIGHT ½-CUP SERVINGS

SPICED GELATO

This gelato uses some of the most popular baking spices—cinnamon, nutmeg, and cloves. It is an ultra-rich ice cream that you'll need an ice cream maker to prepare.

2 EGGS	1 CUP MILK
4 EGG YOLKS	1 TEASPOON CINNAMON
1 CUP SUGAR	½ TEASPOON NUTMEG
2 CUPS HEAVY CREAM	½ TEASPOON CLOVES

1. In a medium mixing bowl, whisk eggs and egg yolks until thick. Add sugar. Beat until light. Add heavy cream, milk, cinnamon, nutmeg, and cloves. Cover with plastic wrap and refrigerate for 2 to 3 hours.

2. Transfer the mixture to an ice cream maker. Follow the manufacturer's instructions for freezing. Place ice cream in an airtight container and freeze until serving. Store in freezer. Serve frozen.

YIELD: ABOUT 1 QUART, 8 SERVINGS

FRUIT
DESSERTS

Fruit and cheese make a great, simple, rustic Italian dessert. I love its simplicity. The recipes in this section offer a variety of fruit prepared in several easy ways, each one not too sweet. Many of these desserts can be made ahead of dinner or can be cooking while you're making dinner. Most are perfect on their own with coffee or a sweet dessert wine.

If you'd like to try a fruit and cheese plate for dessert, try one of these cheeses.

BEL PAESE: A soft mild cheese, perfect with a slice of sweet fruit or sweet bread.

GORGONZOLA: A pungent cheese veined with blue is perfect with fresh figs or apples.

PROVOLONE: A sharp firm cheese great paired with pears or peaches.

RICOTTA: Just a few tablespoons of creamy ricotta and a ripe banana are a simple, satisfying way to end a meal.

BAKED PEARS

PERE AL FORNO

Butter, sugar, and a splash of orange liqueur enhance the flavor of ripened pears for this easy dessert. I like to make this for company if I'm serving pasta for dinner—I use the top of the stove for the pasta and the oven for dessert.

3 RIPE PEARS, HALVED, PEELED, AND CORED

1 TABLESPOON BUTTER

4 TABLESPOONS SUGAR

½ CUP HEAVY CREAM

¼ CUP GRAND MARNIER OR OTHER ORANGE LIQUEUR

1. Preheat oven to 400°F.

2. Place pears, cut side up, in a buttered baking dish. To make the pears lie flat in the baking dish, slice a small part off the rounded side. Dot each half with butter. Sprinkle with sugar. Pour heavy cream and orange liqueur over pears.

3. Bake for 30 to 35 minutes, or until tender.

4. Remove from the oven. Serve warm with excess sauce poured over pears.

YIELD: 6 PEAR HALVES, ABOUT 4 SERVINGS

POACHED PEACHES

This simple dessert is a classic finale to an Italian meal. By absorbing the wine, the peaches take on a delicate sweetness. I enjoy these served warm plain or over ice cream.

2 CUPS WATER

1 CUP SUGAR

3 PEACHES, HALVED, PITTED, AND
PEELED

½ CUP MARSALA WINE, OR ANY SWEET
WHITE WINE

1. In a medium saucepan, bring 2 cups water to a boil over medium heat. Add sugar. Boil until sugar is dissolved, about 3 minutes. Add peaches. Cover and simmer over low heat until peaches are tender, 10 to 15 minutes.

2. Remove from the heat. Stir in wine. Let sit for 15 to 20 minutes. Serve warm or cool.

YIELD: 6 PEACH HALVES, ABOUT 4 SERVINGS

GROWING UP WE ALWAYS HAD PLENTY OF FRUIT IN THE HOUSE. EVERY OTHER MORNING, NICK, OUR PRODUCE MAN, WOULD COME TO SEE MY MOM, AUNTS, AND GRANDMOTHER, WHO ALL LIVED IN THE NEIGHBORHOOD. HE WOULD SIT AND HAVE COFFEE WITH US AND READ THROUGH THE LIST OF WHAT FRUITS AND VEGETABLES HE HAD AVAILABLE THAT DAY ON THE TRUCK. IT WASN'T UNTIL YEARS LATER THAT I REALIZED NOT EVERYONE BOUGHT THEIR PRODUCE THAT WAY.

FRUIT FRITTERS

SFINGI DI FRUTTA

Any firm fruit can be dipped in this batter and fried, but apples are my personal favorite. You can use any variety of apple. For flavor and texture, I prefer McIntosh.

3 EGGS	2 CUPS FLOUR
¼ CUP SUGAR	OIL FOR FRYING
1 CUP MILK	3 MEDIUM APPLES, PEELED, CORED, AND SLICED INTO WEDGES
½ TEASPOON BAKING POWDER	

1. In a medium mixing bowl with wire whisk, beat eggs. Add sugar and milk and mix well. Add baking powder and flour and beat with whisk to make a smooth batter.

2. Heat 1 inch of vegetable oil in a medium saucepan over medium heat. When oil is ready, dip slices of apples into batter, using your fingers, a fork, or tongs. Coat the slice thoroughly and let excess batter fall back into the rest of the batter. Release into oil. Fry the apple slices, a few at a time, without crowding the pan. Turn with two forks or a slotted spoon. Fry until golden brown.

3. Remove from oil and drain on absorbent paper.

4. Sprinkle with cinnamon and sugar or confectioners' sugar, if desired. Serve warm.

YIELD: ABOUT 16 SLICES

MACERATED FRUIT

MACEDONIE

This mixed fruit cup is popular all over Italy. You can use any combination of available fruit and you can substitute a liqueur in place of the wine to suit your taste.

GRATED RIND OF 1 LEMON	½ CANTALOUPE, DICED
GRATED RIND OF 1 ORANGE	1 CUP RED GRAPES (1 SMALL BUNCH)
JUICE OF 1 ORANGE	¼ CUP SUGAR
JUICE OF 1 LEMON	½ CUP WHITE WINE
2 MEDIUM APPLES, PEELED, CORED, AND DICED	1 PINT STRAWBERRIES (1½ CUPS, SLICED)

1. In a large mixing bowl, combine lemon and orange rind and juice, apples, cantaloupe, and grapes. Sprinkle with sugar. Pour over white wine. Stir with a wooden spoon to mix. Cover and refrigerate for 4 to 6 hours before serving. Stir every half hour.

2. Add strawberries right before serving. Spoon into bowls for serving.

YIELD: 6 ½-CUP SERVINGS

◆ MACEDONIE ◆

MACEDONIE IS A TERM USED IN ITALY TO DESCRIBE MIXED FRUIT THAT IS SOAKED WITH SUGAR AND SOME TYPE OF ALCOHOL. LIKE THE COUNTRY OF MACEDONIA, WHERE MANY CULTURES COME TOGETHER, IT'S A COLORFUL, VARIED SPECIALTY.

OTHER FAVORITES

This section includes desserts that are hard to classify. They are casual desserts, such as tiramisù and panna cotta, that are "spooned" out for servings. I've also included pignoli brittle and candied citrus rinds. These are technically candies but are delicious sweets to prepare for yourself or to give as gifts. I've added the popular cordial *limoncello* to round out the book—just as many Italians celebrate the end of a wonderful meal.

CLASSIC TIRAMISÙ

This popular Italian dessert is espresso-soaked savoiardi *(ladyfingers) layered with a mascarpone cheese filling and topped with cocoa. It's assembled like a trifle and very easy to make. After assembling, let the tiramisù set in the refrigerator overnight. It really tastes better when the flavors have a chance to ripen.*

¾ CUP HEAVY CREAM

8 OUNCES MASCARPONE CHEESE

½ CUP SUGAR

1 TABLESPOON COFFEE LIQUEUR

16 SAVOIARDI (LADYFINGERS) (SEE PAGE 37)

1½ CUPS STRONGLY BREWED ESPRESSO

2 TABLESPOONS COCOA

1. In an electric mixer on high speed, beat the cream until thickened. Add mascarpone cheese, sugar, and coffee liqueur. Beat until stiff. Set aside.

2. Line the bottom of an 8-inch square baking dish with a single layer of savoiardi. They can overlap slightly. Place the bottom of the cookie facing up. This is the spongier side that will absorb the espresso. Pour half the espresso over the savoiardi to soak them.

3. Spread half the mascarpone mixture over the soaked savoiardi. Place another single layer of savoiardi on top of mascarpone mixture. Gently press down with your fingers. Soak with remaining espresso. Spread remaining mascarpone mixture on top. Sprinkle with cocoa. Cover with plastic wrap and refrigerate. Serve chilled

YIELD: ABOUT 8 SERVINGS

VARIATION: CHOCOLATE BERRY TIRAMISÙ

Follow recipe for tiramisù. Add ¾ cup cocoa to the mascarpone mixture. Spread ½ cup fresh raspberries over the first layer of mascarpone filling and ½ cup sliced strawberries on next layer of mascarpone.

CINNAMON RICE WITH MILK

This is my grandmother's loose rice pudding that she always made to celebrate the Assumption of Mary, August 15. This recipe works best with traditional long-grain rice, not the converted or minute rice varieties.

3 CUPS WATER

1 CUP LONG GRAIN RICE

2 TABLESPOONS SUGAR

2 CUPS MILK

1 TEASPOON CINNAMON

1. In a medium saucepan, bring water to a boil over medium-high heat. Add rice. Cook uncovered, stirring occasionally, until al dente, about 20 minutes. Remove from the heat. Drain.

2. Sprinkle rice with sugar and mix with a wooden spoon to blend. Let cool slightly.

3. Add milk and transfer mixture to a medium serving bowl. Sprinkle with cinnamon. Do not mix in. Serve warm or refrigerate and serve chilled.

YIELD: EIGHT ½-CUP SERVINGS

◆ RICE ◆

RICE IS USED IN MANY WAYS IN ITALIAN COOKING—IN RICE PIES AND PUDDINGS AND OTHER SAVORY DISHES. MANY BELIEVE THIS IS BECAUSE RICE IS A SYMBOL OF ABUNDANCE AND FERTILITY. IT IS SAID THIS IS WHY WE THROW RICE AT WEDDINGS.

COOKED CREAM

PANNA COTTA

This baked cream is the perfect pudding-like dessert. It's just the right thing when you want a little something sweet. Serve it plain, sprinkled with cinnamon, or garnished with fresh fruit.

1 CUP MILK	½ CUP SUGAR
3 TEASPOONS UNFLAVORED GELATIN	2 TABLESPOONS AMARETTO
3 CUPS HEAVY CREAM	

1. Spray a 9-inch deep-dish Pyrex pie plate or individual ramekins with a nonstick cooking spray. Set aside.

2. Place ½ cup milk in a small bowl. Sprinkle gelatin over milk. Let stand for 10 minutes to soften.

3. In a medium saucepan, combine remaining milk, cream, and sugar. Over medium heat, heat until boiling. Remove from the heat. Add gelatin mixture. Whisk until dissolved. Stir in amaretto.

4. Cool to room temperature, stirring occasionally.

5. Pour into prepared pan or ramekins. Cover with plastic wrap. Refrigerate for 5 hours or overnight.

6. Loosen edges with knife and turn upside down to remove from pan or ramekins.

7. Top with fresh berries or cinnamon and serve.

YIELD: ONE 9-INCH PANNA COTTA, ABOUT 8 SERVINGS

CANDIED CITRUS PEEL

These addictive little treats can be made from any citrus rind—oranges, lemons, or limes. They're like really fresh gumdrops that you can eat by themselves or use as a garnish for a special dessert, like a cassata. Huge piles of them sparkle in the sunny windows of Sicilian pastry shops.

4 ORANGES	2 CUPS SUGAR
3 CUPS WATER	ADDITIONAL SUGAR TO COAT RIND

1. Using a small sharp paring knife, remove rind from the orange. Score the orange rind into fourths and use your fingers to peel off rind. Cut rind, with pith, into slices.

2. Place pieces in a medium saucepan. Cover with 3 cups of water.

3. Boil on high heat for about 15 minutes. Add sugar and boil until thick, syrupy, and reduced, about 20 minutes. Remove from the heat. Drain pieces in strainer and quickly roll them in sugar. Use two forks to toss and coat. Store in an airtight container at room temperature.

YIELD: 1¼ POUNDS

PIGNOLI NUT BRITTLE

Like a tasty Italian peanut brittle, this is great for munching and lasts for weeks. It's delicious served alone as a candy or broken into pieces and sprinkled over your favorite ice cream. This recipe uses pine nuts but you can substitute any of your favorite nuts.

½ CUP PINE NUTS   3 TABLESPOONS WATER

½ CUP SUGAR

1. Preheat oven to 400°F.

2. Spread pine nuts in a thin layer on a parchment-lined cookie sheet. Toast in the oven for 8 to 10 minutes, or until golden brown. Remove from the oven. Set aside to cool.

3. Line another cookie sheet with parchment. Set aside.

4. In a small saucepan over low heat, combine sugar and water. Do not stir. When golden brown, remove from heat. Stir in nuts. Immediately spread nut mixture in a thin layer on lined cookie sheet. Cool. When cool, break into pieces. Store in an airtight container at room temperature.

YIELD: ½ POUND, ABOUT 6 SERVINGS

ROASTED CHESTNUTS

CASTAGNE

Roasted chestnuts are a real winter treat in Italy. You can pick up a handful from a street vendor for a between-meal snack. Our family usually serves them on Sundays and holidays—after dinner, but before dessert.

1 POUND CHESTNUTS (ABOUT 25)

1. Preheat oven to 400°F.

2. Slit chestnuts. Using a small sharp paring knife, cut a small "x" into the chestnut, going through the outer shell and inner skin. Place on a cookie sheet.

3. Bake for 30 to 35 minutes. Cooking time will vary according to the size of chestnuts and personal preference of softness. I like mine al dente. The best way to check doneness is to take a chestnut out of the oven and try it.

4. Remove chestnuts from the oven. Serve hot. Use a pot holder or cloth napkin to break open chestnuts.

YIELD: ABOUT 25 CHESTNUTS

HOMEMADE LIMONCELLO

Limoncello is a delicious and potent digestive cordial that is very popular in Italy.
We always keep a bottle and a few cordial glasses in the freezer because it's best served
ice-cold in a chilled glass. This cordial originated in Capri and we had some
difficulty trying to find it in the United States. Luckily, our friend Luciano,
who lives in Rome, shared his recipe.

750 MILLILITERS GRAIN ALCOHOL	750 MILLILITERS WATER
RIND OF 8 LEMONS	1 POUND SUGAR

1. Combine grain alcohol with grated rind in a large glass sealable container. Store in a cool, dry, dark place for 1 week.

2. Heat water and sugar in a medium saucepan over medium heat. Heat until sugar dissolves and is just about boiling. Remove from the heat.

3. Pour into alcohol mixture. Return mixture to a dark cool place for an additional week.

4. Strain mixture through a fine mesh strainer.

5. Pour into two 750 ml bottles. Cap tightly and store in the freezer. Serve in chilled cordial glasses.

YIELD: TWO 750 ML BOTTLES

◆ Cordials ◆

Sweet liqueurs often accompany desserts in Italy. Sweet wines such as marsala are delicious chilled and sipped. Grappa is a popular liqueur that is made from the skins and seeds of the grapes after the wine is made. Anisette and Sambuca get their anise flavor from the fennel plant, or *finocchio*. Amaretto is a blend of secret herbs and apricot kernels. Strega and Galiano are two popular drinks that are very potent and a striking bright yellow. Many popular Italian cordials are made from age-old secret recipes that include a multitude of herbs and spices.

DESSERT SAUCES

ORANGE SAUCE

This orange sauce enhances an orange dessert or accents a chocolate, mocha, or cheese dessert.

1 CUP ORANGE JUICE   1 TABLESPOON CORNSTARCH
1 CUP CONFECTIONERS' SUGAR

Heat all ingredients in a small saucepan. Whisk until boiling. Boil for 2 minutes, then remove from heat. Let cool. Store in an airtight container in the refrigerator.

RASPBERRY OR
STRAWBERRY SAUCE

This versatile berry sauce is great poured over cakes or ice cream.

2 CUPS RASPBERRIES OR STRAWBER-
RIES, FRESH OR FROZEN (IF USING
FROZEN, LET THEM THAW SLIGHTLY)

1 CUP CONFECTIONERS' SUGAR

In a food processor, pulse berries and sugar until smooth. Store refrigerated in an airtight container.

CHOCOLATE SAUCE

This rich chocolate sauce should be a part of every baker's repertoire.

¼ POUND BUTTER

¾ CUP SUGAR

¾ CUP HEAVY CREAM

½ CUP COCOA POWDER

In a small saucepan, combine butter, sugar, cream, and cocoa. Bring to a boil, stirring constantly until butter melts. Stir until completely blended. Let cool and thicken before use. Store refrigerated in an airtight container. To reheat and thin, heat over simmering water in a double boiler.

YIELD: ABOUT 2 CUPS

INDEX

Lenten biscuits (quaresimali), 18

Limoncello, homemade, 147

Liqueurs and extracts, 4

Little mouthfuls (bocconcini), 105–6

M

Macedonie (macerated fruit), 138

Macerated fruit (macedonie), 138

Making a "well," 8

Mandarin orange meringue cake, 72

Marsala wine, 148

Meringue cake, mandarin orange, 72

Meringues
    almond, 19
    cocoa almond, 20

Millefoglie (thousand-layer apricot cake), 69

Mixers, kitchen, 6

Mocha cream puffs (bigne), 99–100

Molasses nut slices, 26

N

Neapolitan cake, 67–8

Nut cake (torte di noci), 47–8

Nut and jelly crescents, 14

Nuts, 3–4
    toasting, 4

O

Orange cake, Aunt Giulia's (torte d'arancia), 61–2

Orange clove biscotti, 25

Orange confectioners' icing, 17

Orange drop cookies (anginetti d'arancia), 16

Orange sauce, 149

Other dessert favorites, 139–48
    candied citrus peel, 144
    castagne (roasted chestnuts), 146
    cinnamon rice with milk, 142
    cooked cream (panna cotta), 143
    chocolate berry tiramisù, 141
    classic tiramisù, 141
    general information about, 140
    homemade limoncello, 147
    panna cotta (cooked cream), 143
    pignoli nut brittle, 145
    roasted chestnuts (castagne), 146

Ovens, 6–7

P

Pane d'anise (anise bread), 116

Pane di Pasqua (Easter bread), 17–18

Pane di Pasqua con uovo (braided Easter bread with eggs), 119–20

Pane di spagna (sponge cake), 46

Panettone (Christmas fruit bread), 121–2

Panna cotta (cooked cream), 143

Parchment, 6

Pasta frolla (tender pie dough), 78

Pastry, 97–111
    bigne (mocha cream puffs), 99–100
    bocconcini (little mouthfuls), 105–6
    butterflies (farfalle), 107
    fig and mascarpone ravioli, 111
    general information about, 98
    lemon ricotta fritters (sfingi di ricotta), 108
    little mouthfuls (bocconcini), 105–6
    mocha cream puffs (bigne), 99–100
    pasticiotte, 109–10
    rum sponge cake, 103–4
    sfingi di ricotta (lemon ricotta fritters), 108
    traditional cannoli, 101–2